THE FRENCH REVOLUTION

Notes on References

References are cited throughout in brackets according to the numbering in the general bibliography, with page references where necessary indicated by a colon after the bibliography number.

Editor's Preface

The main purpose of this series is to make available to teacher and student alike developments in a field of history that has become increasingly specialised with the sheer volume of new research and literature now produced. These studies are designed to present the state of the debate on important themes and episodes in European history since the sixteenth century, presented in a clear and critical way by someone who is closely concerned with the debate in question.

The studies are not intended to be read as extended bibliographical essays, though each will contain a detailed guide to further reading which will lead students and the general reader quickly to key publications. Each book carries its own interpretation and conclusions, while locating the discussion firmly in the centre of the current issues as historians see them. It is intended that the series will introduce students to historical approaches which are in some cases very new and which, in the normal course of things, would take many years to filter down into the textbooks and school histories. I hope it will demonstrate some of the excitement historians, like scientists, feel as they work away in the vanguard of their subject.

The format of the series conforms closely with that of the companion volumes of studies in economic and social history which has already established a major reputation since its inception in 1968. Both series have an important contribution to make in publicising what it is that historians are doing and in making history more open and accessible. It is vital for history to communicate if it is to survive.

R. J. OVERY

Introduction

Few if any inaugural lectures can have had the enduring impact of 'The myth of the French Revolution', delivered by the late Alfred Cobban to University College, London, in 1954 [145 (b)]. It marked the beginning of a controversy about the origins, nature and consequences of the French Revolution which has dominated writing on the subject ever since and which shows no signs of flagging. So voluminous has the literature become, that this short book can do no more than outline the present state of hostilities and suggest how further reading might add substance to the sketch offered.

After thirty years of vigorous argument, consensus is as far away as ever. For the supporters of the 'myth' that Cobban was attacking, the old view still stands like a *rocher de bronze*, despite all the revisionist criticism which has washed around it. In the defiant first words of a recent general history of post-revolutionary France: 'Despite recent attempts by French, British and American writers to reinterpret the French Revolution, the only plausible, coherent analysis remains that of scholars who, in the tradition of the great French historian Georges Lefebvre, see it as a "bourgeois Revolution"' [180]. Compare that with the equally confident, and even more recent, pronouncement in the volume in the same series which deals with the revolutionary-Napoleonic period: 'Research and reflective criticism over the past twenty years have rendered the classical [Marxist] view of the origins of the Revolution utterly untenable' [12]. As the firmness – not to say trenchancy – of these and a host of other similar verdicts suggests, the controversy has been a dialogue of the deaf.

If scholars who have devoted their lives to the study of French history in the period cannot reach even a modicum of agreement, passing each other unhailed like ships in the night, one might wonder what mere amateurs can hope to make of it all. As we shall

1

see, in fact it is a game we all can play, for 'solutions' depend less on factual knowledge than on presuppositions about such imprecise matters as the course of modern history, social relationships and human nature. One man's 'fundamental insight' turns out to be another man's 'out-dated shibboleth' – and vice versa.

Our point of entry must be the 'myth' which Cobban was attacking in his inaugural lecture. His target can be termed 'the Marxist interpretation', although – as we shall see later – that convenient label covers several different shades of meaning. Its most succinct formulation can be found in a short but penetrating book by Georges Lefebvre: *The Coming of the French Revolution* [17]. The essential cause of the Revolution he located in a growing discrepancy between public pretension and economic reality. In legal terms, the old regime was dominated by the first two estates: the clergy and the nobility. It was they who occupied the commanding heights of state and society, it was they who enjoyed all the prestige. In feudal society, when land had been virtually the only form of wealth, their privileged position had had a secure economic base, but by the late eighteenth century it had become an anachronism. For by then the development of commerce and industry had created a new class, the bourgeoisie. Increasingly numerous, prosperous and self-confident, their sense of frustration sharpened by the growing exclusiveness of their social superiors ('the aristocratic reaction'), the bourgeois would not tolerate indefinitely their subordinate position: 'Such a discrepancy never lasts for ever. The Revolution of 1789 restored the harmony between fact and law' [17]. Ironically, it was the nobles who thrust the first battering-ram against the old regime, with their suicidal attack on the absolute monarchy in 1787, thus opening the breach through which the bourgeois poured. As Chateaubriand commented: 'The patricians began the Revolution, the plebeians completed it'.

In other words, the French Revolution represented the decisive stage in the progression from feudalism to capitalism and thus to the modern world. Every country in Europe, of course, made this transition at some stage. What made the French version so special – the greatest revolution in the history of the world, in Marx's view – was its speed, violence and completeness. This radicalism it owed to two interrelated developments. Firstly, there was the determined rearguard action fought by the privileged orders and their foreign allies, in the form of counter-revolution at home and war abroad. Secondly, there was the crucial assistance the essentially timid bourgeois received from the urban masses and the peasants. If the bourgeois had had their way, the Revolution would have been closed down by 1791 at the latest. It was only insistent pressure from below which drove them on to destroy feudalism in its entirety [26].

Yet although separate social strands can be identified, they were not discrete entities but were woven into the seamless whole. Like the acts of a play or the movements of a symphony, the peasant or urban revolutions acquired meaning only when seen as parts of the one and indivisible Revolution. As Albert Soboul, Lefebvre's successor as professor of French revolutionary studies at the Sorbonne, wrote: 'There were not three revolutions in 1789, but just the one alone, bourgeois and liberal, with popular support and especially with peasant support' [25]. Although in a subjective sense the masses may have appeared at times anti-capitalist and at odds with the bourgeois leadership, objectively their participation drove the Revolution on to its goal – the elimination of feudalism.

This was no quick or easy process. The bourgeoisie may have claimed to speak in the name of all humanity, proclaiming universal and eternal truths in the Declaration of the Rights of Man and the Citizen in 1789, for example, but in reality their objectives were narrowly circumscribed. Always prone to compromise with the old order, always seeking to frustrate the genuinely egalitarian and democratic aspirations of the masses, as time passed they allowed their naked class-interests to show through the increasingly revealing garb of revolutionary rhetoric. One crucial stage in this ideological striptease was reached with the *coup d'état* of Thermidor in July 1794, when the revolutionary dictatorship of the Committee of Public Safety was overthrown. Another was the recourse to a military saviour in the shape of General Bonaparte in 1799. Neither of those solutions proved permanent. It was not until 1830 and the July Revolution which toppled the last Bourbon that the French bourgeoisie reached safety, by now not even bothering to pretend that they represented anyone but themselves.

3

Against this 'classic interpretation', as Soboul called it, the revisionists have launched a series of attacks. At the outset it must be stressed that not all revisionists would subscribe to every individual point of the summary which follows, necessarily painted with broad brush-strokes. Chronologically, the first target has been the nature of social and economic change during the eighteenth century. That the economy expanded is not questioned; that it intensified class-conflict between the nobility and the bourgeoisie most certainly is. The expansion of capitalist enterprise was not the exclusive achievement of the bourgeoisie; on the contrary, many of the most progressive entrepreneurs were nobles [52]. Most bourgeois proved to be positively timid, preferring to invest their capital in land, seigneuries, venal office and government stock [39]. Low in risk – and low in returns – such investments could open the way to the realisation of every bourgeois' dream: the acquisition of noble status. Far from seeking to fight the nobles, the most earnest wish of the *bourgeois gentilhomme* was to join them. It was not difficult to do so. So many ennobling offices were for sale, that anyone with sufficient funds could make the transition [49]. The result was that the French nobility was very numerous; even if the lowest of many possible estimates is taken, the figure (c. 25,000 families) is more than one hundred times larger than that yielded by the British peerage (220 peers in 1790). Far from being an increasingly closed caste, the French nobility was an open elite – too open for its own good, indeed. The 'aristocratic reaction' was a myth [33].

The revisionists have also stressed the heterogeneity of the nobility and the bourgeoisie. So diverse were the members of each group in terms of wealth, position and outlook that neither constituted a class. On the contrary, the upper echelons of each came together to form a single elite – 'the notables' – united by wealth and talent [36]. As an alternative label – *l'élite des lumières* – suggests, this fusion found ideological expression in the Enlightenment, not the creed or creation of the bourgeoisie but in large measure the work of the liberal nobility.

If relative harmony ruled among the commanding heights of the old regime, why then did it fall? The answer lies in the fortuitous coincidence of two separate crises at the end of the 1780s. They were not 'discrete' in the sense that each was self-sufficient, for they interacted one with the other, but they were essentially separate [38]. The first crisis was political, deriving from the financial bankruptcy of the monarchy following French participation in the American War of Independence. It brought the virtual collapse of royal government by the summer of 1788 and with it the decision to convene the Estates General. The second crisis was economic, stemming most immediately from the general harvest failure of 1788 but with longer-term origins in population pressure and the recession which had begun in the 1770s [1]. It was the fusion of these two crises in the spring and summer of 1789 which allowed the mass of discontents to become critical and to turn a crisis into a revolution.

What then followed was no class struggle between nobility and bourgeoisie, despite the emotive rhetoric of the Revolution's supporters, but a political contest for power. There were relatively few representatives of the financial, commercial and industrial bourgeoisie at the Estates General: the great majority of the Third Estate's deputies were local officials, professional men and, above all, lawyers [145 (b)]. Moreover, the leaders of the National Assembly – which the Estates General became at the end of June – were nobles, not only in 1789 but throughout the most constructive phase of the Revolution. The sort of France they tried to create was certainly tailored to suit the needs of the bourgeoisie, but would have provided an equally snug fit for the enterprising and wealthy nobles too. In short, it was to be a France created by the notables for the notables.

There are several possible explanations for their failure – in the short term, at least – to achieve this goal. There was the artificial division between noble and commoner created by the manner in which the Estates General were organised [36]. There was the unforeseen and unwanted intervention by the masses, which prompted the bourgeoisie to save their own skins by diverting popular fury against the aristocratic scapegoats [30]. There was the temporary inability of both nobles and bourgeois to look beyond rhetoric to their true interests [151]. There were the persistent economic difficulties which kept the pot of social unrest on the boil. Most crucially perhaps, there was the refusal of the king to play the role allocated to him by the notables, which in turn allowed a group of political radicals to take France into a foreign war [142, 143].

None of these explanations are mutually exclusive. Whatever permutation is preferred, the upshot was that the Revolution was 'blown off course' between 1792 and 1794 [6]. With the compass spinning crazily, this sudden squall brought the abolition of the monarchy, the execution of the king and queen, the attack on Catholicism, counter-revolution, both civil and foreign war, revolutionary dictatorship and the Terror. But the *coup d'état* of Thermidor put the notables back on the bridge, this time for good: political forms may have come and gone, but they stayed on for ever [177].

The France they ruled was a country whose economy had changed astonishingly little as a result of the Revolution. The agriculture of the old regime had been characterised by small units, cultivated by peasants aiming only at subsistence; the agriculture of post-revolutionary France was just the same. The manufacturing sector of the old regime had been characterised by small units, staffed by artisans aiming only at local markets; the manufacturing sector of post-revolutionary France was just the same. Indeed, the changes introduced by the Revolution had been retrograde rather than progressive. The land settlement and the laws of inheritance encouraged fragmentation and kept the peasantry on the land. The monetary chaos of the 1790s, the embargo on British technology and the loss of overseas markets slowed industrialisation. The 'expansion' of the first decade of Napoleon's rule represented only recovery, not a new advance. Most damaging of all, the collapse of overseas trade and the loss of overseas colonies brought poverty to the ports of the Atlantic seaboard and deindustrialisation to their hinterlands [146]. 'Economically', William Doyle has commented, 'the Revolution was a disaster for France' [57].

Certainly France did experience, in due course, a process of modernisation which in certain respects can be termed bourgeois – the creation of a national market, urbanisation, industrialisation, mass literacy, and so on – but it did so in spite of, not because of, the revolutionary legacy. The real destroyer of the old regime was not the Revolution but the railway network constructed more than half a century later [57, 184]. Indeed, one influential historian of rural France has dated its transformation to the very end of the nineteenth century [188].

It has been much easier to identify what the French Revolution was *not* than what it actually was. Not unreasonably, Marxists and their sympathisers reacted to their critics by pointing to the essentially negative nature of the revisionist project. If the Revolution was not caused by the tension between the ossified old regime and progressive forces of production, then where *did* it come from? If the Revolution did not represent the victory of the bourgeoisie over the monarchy and the aristocracy, then what *did* it mean? In answer to those questions, some revisionists maintained a prudent silence, while others offered answers as hesitant and qualified as their critiques had been confident and dismissive. It was a major step forward in revisionist historiography, therefore, when François Furet published *Penser la Révolution française* in 1978, translated into English as *Interpreting the French Revolution* two years later [35]. Although this collection of essays included one of the more intemperate (and effective) attacks on Soboul, it also opened the way towards an alternative interpretation which was cultural rather than social. In the last two decades, a growing host of other scholars has followed Furet's example, spurred on by the bicentenary of the fall of the Bastille and the attendant explosion of conferences and publications (no fewer than 170 conferences were held across the world to mark the event in 1988–9). This post-revisionist group concentrates on what has now become a very well-worn concept: 'political culture'. Led by Furet himself, Mona Ozouf, Arlette Farge, Keith Michael Baker, Lynn Hunt, Dena Goodman, Jack Censer, Jeremy Popkin, and Joan Landes – just to mention a few – it has produced myriad studies of the old regime and Revolution whose distinction, originality and sophistication are not always, alas, matched by corresponding clarity and cogency. In particular, one sometimes wonders whether the gorgeous verbiage with which their findings are decked out is supported by an equally muscular body of meaning.

It was doubly unfortunate for the Marxists that just as their intellectual citadel crumbled, so did their contemporary focus of loyalty – the Soviet Union and its empire – collapse. As we shall see, much of the writing about the French Revolution was inspired by the need to seek a historical pedigree for what was thought to be the even greater revolution of 1917. So, once the state created by the Bolsheviks was revealed in all its unpopularity, criminality and impotence, there was less need to cram what evidence could be found of a 'bourgeois revolution' in 1789 into anachronistic categories. But did the cortège which bore Bolshevism to the 'rubbish-tip of history' (to employ one of Lenin's favourite images when

7

describing the destination of anyone who disagreed with him) also take with it the controversy over the bourgeois nature of the French Revolution? This has certainly been the verdict of some historians, who have dismissed it as 'an old debate, which is not worth pursuing' [8]. But this sort of dismissal fails to take account of what Hegel called 'the cunning of history'. In the same way that 1789 did not usher in a new millennium of liberty, equality and fraternity, 1989 was followed not by the universal acceptance of liberal democracy and thus the end of history, but by waves of crime, impoverishment, ethnic cleansing, neo-fascism and civil war. It can only be a matter of time before a de-bolshevised form of Marxism regains its intellectual credibility, not least because of its inherent force.

Moreover, if there is more than one way of killing a cat, there is more than one way of identifying the French Revolution as bourgeois. If the revisionists have had the best of the argument over the past two decades, the social interpretation is resting rather than dying, as the occasional twitch of its limbs indicates [13, 16, 161]. Fortunately for Marxists and others who look to society for the driving forces of history, the course of historiography is not dialectical but cyclical and it will not be long before cultural explanations of the decline and fall of the old regime begin to seem old hat in their turn. There is every reason, therefore, to go on analysing and arguing about the social character of the French Revolution, nòt least because it is a debate which addresses the fundamentals of the history of France and Europe and indeed of historical debate *per se*. On the other hand, this is not to deny that Furet and his followers have greatly enhanced our understanding of the period. Their arguments deserve to be taken seriously, especially now that they have reached maturity. In what follows, therefore, the rise and fall of the social interpretation will be charted and a friendly but critical eye will be cast at the alternatives offered by the exponents of 'political culture'.

1 Origins: the Old Regime

(i) Economic Growth and Economic Problems

'The essential cause of the Revolution', wrote Albert Soboul, 'was the power of a bourgeoisie arrived at its maturity and confronted by a decadent aristocracy holding tenaciously to its privileges' [23]. Born in the first stirrings of a market economy in the middle ages, passing through a troubled adolescence with the overseas discoveries and colonial expansion of the sixteenth and seventeenth centuries, the French bourgeoisie certainly grew in numbers and in wealth in the course of the eighteenth century. The interrelated phenomena of more favourable meteorological conditions, increasing agricultural production and population growth created the necessary conditions for sustained economic expansion.

Beneficent nature was given a helping hand by the state. By providing France with the best network of arterial roads in Europe, so that the time taken to travel from Paris to Lyon, for example, was halved in the course of the eighteenth century, it contributed towards the formation of a national market. By dismantling the restrictive practices of the guilds, it opened the way for capitalist entrepreneurs to exploit growing market opportunities. The rapid expansion of rural industry on a putting-out basis achieved rates of growth comparable to those of Great Britain, even in cottons [54]. Iron production and coal extraction also recorded spectacular percentage increases. Evidence of the international hegemony of the luxury industries of Paris can still be found in every stately home and museum in Europe.

But the real success story of the French economy in the eighteenth century was overseas commerce. In the Mediterranean, French merchants established a near-monopoly of the lucrative trade with the Levant, to such an extent that in 1780 an official memorandum estimated that it sustained between 500,000 and 600,000 people. Even that paled by comparison with the mushrooming colonial sector. From the Atlantic ports, notably Bordeaux, Nantes and Le Havre-Rouen, an ever-increasing merchant marine sailed a triangular route, first to Africa for slaves, and thence to the Caribbean for the colonial produce which fed the apparently insatiable appetites of the rest of Europe. Between the end of the War of the Spanish Succession and the Revolution, French overseas trade at least quadrupled in value, and may have quintupled [54]. Even when the increase in prices, reduction in tariffs and decline in smuggling are taken into account, it can be said that the volume of foreign trade doubled during the same period. Moreover, the expansion of colonial trade was maintained right up until 1789: in 1773 510 ships left eleven French ports for Santo Domingo (by far the most important of the French Caribbean possessions), Martinique, Guadeloupe and Guyana; by 1788 that figure had increased to 686.

But behind these impressive quantitative increases, little if any qualitative change had occurred. Old regime France was a tale of two economies – the prosperous, expanding maritime coasts, together with their shallow hinterlands, and the great mass of the interior, backward, traditionalist and subdivided into largely autarkic local markets [57]. Even the most glamorous sectors, like the colonial re-export trade, did not have sufficient power to draw the rest of the economy into self-sustained growth.

A major obstacle to capital and enterprise flowing from one sector to another was the primitive nature of the financial institutions. For some reason which has never been explained adequately, such modern techniques as bills of exchange, discounting and even double-entry book-keeping came very late to France. More easily explicable, but no less damaging, was the tenacious aversion to banks in the wake of John Law's spectacular bankruptcy in 1720. The old regime knew no state bank, no private bank independent of commerce, no stock exchange and virtually no joint-stock companies [61].

Also structurally backward was the manufacturing sector, whose growth statistics look much less impressive when the low base from which they are calculated is taken into account. And when the techniques of production are examined, the qualitative backwardness of French industry is clearly revealed. By 1789, for example, Great Britain had well over 20,000 spinning jennies, 9,000 of the newer mule jennies and 200 mills on the Arkwright model. The equivalent figures for France were: fewer than a thousand, none and eight. Moreover, the great majority of the French machines had been built under the auspices of the royal government and only for the purposes of attracting the special subsidy on offer [70]. In short, the French economy of 1789 was essentially the same as the French economy of 1715 – it was just producing more [54]. Nor was it a story of consistent success even in a purely quantitative sense. Increasing competition from Britain and Central Europe (especially Silesia and Saxony), the protectionist policies adopted by old customers such as Spain and the domestic recession beginning in the 1770s all conspired to send the French textile industry into the Revolution in a debilitated state [48].

Given that some 85 per cent of the French population lived in the countryside, more important was the backward state of agriculture. As the most authoritative estimate suggests that the total population increased from around 22 million in 1700 to around 28 million in 1789 [58] it is evident that there must have been some increase in production. At one time it was argued that this increase was in the order of 60 per cent – about double the rate of population growth – but more recent estimates (and the lack of reliable statistics make them largely a matter of guesswork) place it very much lower [60]. Great or small, most of it was due to an expansion of the acreage cultivated, to previously waste land being put under the plough, not to any rise in *productivity*. Most of French agriculture remained locked in the 'infernal circle of the fallow' (land left fallow = low productivity = high percentage of arable = low percentage of pasture = insufficient livestock = insufficient manure = need for fallow). In 1760 the agronomist Duhamel de Monceau complained that 'almost half the land in this kingdom lies fallow, the other half is generally so badly cultivated that it would bring in at least twice as much if it were properly exploited' [138].

Any landowner or cultivator with sufficient knowledge, capital and enterprise to break out of the circle by the introduction of new crops and new rotations found his way barred by two formidable obstacles. The first was the *servitudes collectives*, the obligation to plant, till, harvest and graze as a community, which ensured that it moved at the pace of its slowest member, i.e. not at

11

all. Sporadic attempts by the government to encourage innovation made little impression [50]. The other obstacle – the inadequacy of communications – was, if anything, more serious and more intractable. Before the railways came, the only cost-efficient way to move grain was by navigable waterways, an asset the French interior notably lacked. It has been estimated that food could not be moved overland further than fifteen kilometres before transport costs devoured the profit margin [184]. The result was wasteful polyculture and an inability to specialise in those crops best suited to a region's soil and climate: for example, in 1789 wine was produced in all but three of the thirty-two *généralités* into which the country was divided [184].

Within this unpromising framework, there was little opportunity and less incentive to engage in the agricultural modernisation needed to allow industrialisation. This picture of rural stagnation should not be overdrawn. In parts of the South-West the introduction of maize allowed yields to be increased; in the North and East – and especially around large towns – new crops were introduced and the fallow eliminated [57]. Not for the first or last time, it is necessary to remind oneself that France was an aggregate of many different economies. Nevertheless, even when the last exception has been noted, the contrast with the agriculture of the Low Countries and Great Britain is very striking.

For the purposes of our present concern, the most important difference lay in the attitude of the landowners. Although improving landlords were to be found, appreciating that a rich tenant meant a rich proprietor, the rate of long-term reinvestment of rural incomes appears to have been low [57]. With market opportunities limited by the inhibiting factors discussed earlier, and with population pressure creating an ever-lengthening queue of would-be tenants and share-croppers, the easy way to extra income was through smaller plots and higher rents [62].

So the French economy in the eighteenth century remained predominantly traditional and it is difficult to see how 'the power of a bourgeoisie arrived at its maturity' (see above, p. 9) could be identified within it. It proves even more difficult when the actual aspirations of the bourgeois are considered. It was not the capitalist sectors of the economy which attracted them but the essentially non-capitalist forms of 'proprietary wealth' – land, urban property, venal offices and government stock. It was the first of those – land – which appealed most, partly for its security but mainly for the prestige it conveyed. The bourgeois used their money to buy land which would yield just 1 or 2 per cent, instead of depositing it with merchants who would pay 5 per cent; and they borrowed at 5 per cent to buy land . . . which would yield only 1 or 2 per cent [39]. It has been estimated that at least 80 per cent of the private wealth of France was proprietary in character. Even in the most commercialised of cities it was preponderant: at Bordeaux, for example, there were 700 merchants, brokers and manufacturers, but 1,100 officials, rentiers and property-owners – and many of the merchants held much of their wealth in proprietary form [39].

The other side of the coin was a striking number of enterprising, innovative noble capitalists. Especially from the 1770s they became 'massively involved' in overseas trading companies and heavy industry [52]. Far from being feudal relics chained to traditional forms of wealth, it was they who were setting the pace in promoting economic change: 'in its most modernising aspects, commercial capitalism was more in the hands of nobles than of bourgeois' [30].

(ii)   Social Conflict and Social Fusion

With so many bourgeois behaving like nobles and so many nobles behaving like bourgeois, it is difficult to find much evidence of class conflict between the two. Indeed it is difficult to identify them as classes at all, whether one adopts a Marxist definition of class based on economic function and class consciousness or a more general definition such as that proposed by Marc Bloch, who wrote that he would consider those people to be of the same class 'whose ways of life were sufficiently similar and whose material circumstances were sufficiently close not to create any conflict of interest' [47]. No one knows just how many nobles there were, estimates ranging from as low as 100,000 to as high as 400,000. As the apparently endless variety unfolds – among other differences, French nobles could be as poor as church-mice and as rich as Croesus – one can answer in the affirmative Robert Forster's question: 'should we not go a step further and abandon "nobility" altogether as a social category?' [177].

Also ripe for rejection is the notion that the nobility engaged in an 'aristocratic reaction' in the eighteenth century, thus sharpening the bourgeoisie's sense of frustration. Certainly nobles dominated government, administration, the church and the most important social institutions – but they had always done so [33]. If anything, the trend was towards preferring nobles of more recent origin. Where it occurred – and it was not general – the upward revision of seigneurial dues owed more to commercialisation (new investments) than to any feudal initiative [31]. Measures which at first sight betray noble exclusiveness turn out to have been aimed not at non-nobles but at *other* nobles. A classic case was the notorious 'Ségur ordinance' of 1781 which confined admission to the officer corps to nobles with four generations of noble status behind them. This represented a move on behalf of the poor provincial nobility, for whom the army was the chief source of employment, against well-heeled *anoblis* who bought their way up the promotion ladder [49].

This episode highlighted the most corrosive social conflict within the old regime and the most damaging failure of the monarchy. The two most successful and stable states of eighteenth-century Europe – Great Britain and Prussia – owed their success and stability to the integration of their elites, albeit achieved in two very different ways. The task had been facilitated by those elites' relative homogeneity. In France, Louis XIV's creation of an exclusive court, imposition of centralisation and massive expansion of ennobling venal office had saddled the monarchy with a nobility which was too numerous, too diverse and too unintegrated. Languishing in provincial penury and obscurity, the lesser nobility harboured intense resentment of the magnates of the court. Many of them – perhaps as many as a quarter – were too poor even to raise the modest sums required for entry to military service. Their chances of gaining admission to the charmed circles of the magnates were negligible (it was far easier for the daughter of a wealthy *anobli* to marry into a great family than for the daughter of a country squire, however ancient his lineage) [52].

Together with the demoralisation resulting from the monarchy's failures in the course of the eighteenth century, most notably in the all-important fields of war and foreign policy, this growing resentment left the regime friendless when disaster struck at the end of the 1780s. When Louis XVI reached for what should have been his most loyal and most potent weapon – the army – in the summer of 1789, it fell apart in his hands [143].

If anything, the bourgeoisie was even more fissiparous. If it is thought to have been growing rapidly – it may have trebled between 1660 and 1789 [57] – this is due in part to its portmanteau character. For contemporaries, a 'bourgeois' could be a town-dweller, a rentier, a member of the Third Estate, an *anobli*, an economically active and independent commoner, or just a 'boss' [2]. Far from being identified with economically progressive groups, the term was often associated with a person of independent means, as opposed to an active entrepreneur [59]. Of course Marxists are well aware of this diversity: Georges Lefebvre identified five groups (rentiers; officials and lawyers; financiers, shipowners, merchants and manufacturers; artisans and tradesmen; intellectuals, journalists, musicians, artists, etc.); Albert Soboul found four (rentiers; the liberal professions; artisans and shopkeepers; businessmen) [18, 24]. Nevertheless, they are insistent that essentially all these groups constituted a single class:

> Without doubt the bourgeoisie was diverse and manifold: a social class is rarely homogeneous. But the bourgeoisie was also *one* . . . Top of the list of bourgeois criteria was without any doubt fortune, not so much by virtue of its size as by virtue of its origins, its form, the manner in which it was administered and spent: 'to live like a bourgeois'. There can be no doubt that a Frenchman of the eighteenth century could tell without difficulty whether such and such a person belonged to the aristocracy or stemmed from the bourgeoisie [25].

But even if Soboul's own criteria are adopted, it is difficult to see how his four categories can be made to form a single class – for the origin, form, management and spending of the fortunes of rentiers, the liberal professions, artisans, shopkeepers and businessmen patently were not '*one*' but very different. The fact of the matter is that the 'bourgeoisie' is a convenient – not to say indispensable – term to designate those commoners who were neither peasants nor labourers, but it did not constitute a class.

Soboul's insistence on the modernity of the leading sector of the bourgeoisie and the confrontational nature of its relationship with the nobility has been criticised by other Marxist historians with a more subtle approach. Régine Robin, for example, has argued that there is more than one way to kill a cat – and more than one route from feudalism to capitalism. More convincing than the class-war model advocated by Soboul and his followers, she suggests, is to see the transition as a process of 'intermingling' (*intrication*). Before 1789 the relations of production were being transformed in 'the Prussian way', as feudal exploitation made way for capitalist exploitation with the old elites still in place. Such a pattern is entirely compatible with Marxist theory and, ironically, can accommodate without strain the empirical research of revisionists seeking to deny the validity of that theory. It was Soboul's mistake to try to keep the Revolution as the centre of the transition from feudalism to capitalism and thus to distort its significance [15].

From a rather different – but also Marxist – perspective, Louis Althusser also sought to account for the lack of antagonism between nobility and bourgeoisie during the old regime. He argued that the *industrial* bourgeoisie – 'the true modern bourgeoisie, which transformed the previous economic and social orders from top to bottom' – was unknown to the eighteenth century. Then the most advanced sector was a bourgeoisie which depended on the *mercantile* economy and which consequently was a well-integrated part of the feudal order, with no ambition to fight it. On the contrary, when it acquired wealth, it used it for the purchase of land, venal office, government stock – and noble status. So the order of battle pitched not absolute monarchy against nobles, or nobles against bourgeois, but the feudal regime in its entirety against the masses it exploited. There was a theoretical dispute between king, nobility and bourgeoisie, but a social conflict between the regime and the masses [92]. In fact, as we shall see later, this emphasis on the revolutionary role of the masses accords well with another of Soboul's central arguments.

Whatever one's theoretical point of departure, it is clear that far from fighting the nobles, the bourgeois sought to join them. It was easy to do so – provided the aspirant had enough money. The quickest route was through the purchase of the position of 'King's Secretary', a venal sinecure which conferred immediate and hereditary nobility on the purchaser and his family. Despite the cost – as high as 150,000 livres by the end of the old regime – there were around 2,500 takers (including Voltaire and

Beaumarchais) in the course of the eighteenth century [52, 74]. There was a host of other venal offices conferring nobility, although most of them did so only after a period of time. It has been estimated that at least 6,500 families acquired nobility in the course of the century; in other words, about a quarter of the total French nobility was of very recent origin. Significantly, the largest group of these *anoblis* consisted of great merchants, financiers and manufacturers [52]. Neither was there any sign that the urge to social advancement was fading, for between the accession of Louis XVI in 1774 and 1789, 2,477 individuals (including 878 who bought King's Secretaryships) made the leap [49].

These statistics constitute relatively 'hard' evidence of the eagerness of the upper echelons of the bourgeoisie to amalgamate with the nobility. More elusive is the evidence of the reverse process. Revisionists such as Chaussinand-Nogaret insist that it was not just a case of the aristocratisation of the bourgeoisie, but also of the embourgeoisement of the nobility:

> From 1760 onward the notions of worthiness and honour, which until then had defined what was special about nobles, were overtaken by a new notion: merit, a middle class value, typical of the third order, which nobility took over, made its own, accepted and officially recognised as a criterion of nobility. From that moment on there was no longer any significant difference between nobility and middle classes. A noble was now nothing but a commoner who had made it [52].

Such a broad generalisation about such a large number of people is necessarily difficult to substantiate. As we shall see later, the most convincing evidence is retrospective, stemming from the remarkable similarity of the *cahiers de doléances* compiled by the nobility and the Third Estate for the Estates General in 1789. Before that episode can be considered, it is necessary to turn to their joint participation in the progressive cultural movement of the eighteenth century, to the Enlightenment.

(iii)   The Enlightenment

In the context of this study, two main questions concern us: can the Enlightenment be termed 'bourgeois'? and what was the rela-

tionship between the Enlightenment and the French Revolution?
Most Marxist historians give an unequivocal answer to the first: 'In
the perspective of social history, the Enlightenment is a histori-
cally important stage in the development of western bourgeois
thought'. The central ideas of the Enlightenment are identified
and are found to correspond to the essential characteristics of the
market economy which produced the bourgeoisie. So, for Lucien
Goldmann, for example, the principal mental categories needed
in a society based on exchange are individualism, contract, equality, universality, toleration, freedom and property, and 'anyone
who knows the eighteenth century in France will see that this list
(and it is no coincidence) is identical with the fundamental categories of the thought of the Enlightenment'.

This sort of bird's-eye view, *sub specie aeternitatis*, can accommodate – on its own terms, at least – all the awkward irregularities in
the terrain revealed when the focus of vision shifts closer to
ground-level. No matter that the philosophes were heterogeneous
both ideologically and socially, no matter that large sections of the
bourgeoisie were indifferent or hostile to the Enlightenment,
essentially 'the history of social thought in France in the eighteenth century is above all the history of the development and diffusion of bourgeois ideology and the history of the ideological
preparation of the bourgeois revolution' [29]. Not for the first or
last time, we reach a point at which mere argument can make no
further progress – it becomes a matter of faith. All that can be
done is to draw attention to the most important qualifications
which suggest that the French Enlightenment did not have a single social identity.

The first place to look, clearly, is at the background of the
philosophes. Of course, an examination of a man's social origins
provides an inadequate guide to the social nature of his thoughts
– the fact that Lenin, for example, came from the nobility hardly
justifies labelling Marxism-Leninism as aristocratic. But it does
help somewhat. If *all* the philosophes had been bourgeois, the
sweeping generalisations such as those by Goldmann and
Volguine quoted earlier would be easier to swallow. In the event,
one has to choke on discovering that so many of them –
Montesquieu, Mably, Jaucourt, Condorcet, Condillac,
Vauvenargues, Buffon, Helvétius, Lavoisier, Quesnay, Turgot,
Mirabeau (among others) – were nobles. Others turned their

backs on their origins by buying their way into the nobility [74]. The list of contributors to the most important single work of the French Enlightenment – *L'Encyclopédie* – includes a high proportion of nobles old and new, a surprising number of clergymen (12 per cent) and in general reveals a cross-section of the upper and middle classes [113]. Moreover, it has been argued that by the 1780s all the leading lights had been safely assimilated into the high society of the old regime.

If the producers did not form a coherent bloc, neither did the consumers. The *Encyclopédie* did not appeal to the economically progressive sectors of French society, but to the traditional elites – nobles, officials, lawyers and clergymen. Besançon, an old-fashioned provincial capital, with a population of 28,000, provided 338 subscribers to the quarto edition; Lille, an expanding manufacturing centre, with a population of 61,000, provided just twenty-eight. As Robert Darnton concludes: 'The readers of the book came from the sectors of society that were to crumble quickest in 1789, from the world of parlements and bailliages, from the Bourbon bureaucracy and the army and the church' [97].

Similar results have been yielded by quantitative studies of two of the main institutional centres of enlightened activity – the provincial academies and the masonic lodges. In the former, 20 per cent of the members were clergymen, 37 per cent nobles and 43 per cent bourgeois. Most of the bourgeois, moreover, were medical men, lawyers, writers and teachers; merchants and businessmen were notably under-represented. The Freemasons were certainly more bourgeois in character, the share of the clergy dropping to 4 per cent and that of the nobility to 15 per cent (22 per cent in Paris). And here, at last, some capitalist bourgeois are to be found, for 36 per cent of the masons in the provinces (17 per cent in Paris) were from banking, commerce or manufacturing. Much work of this kind remains to be done, but it seems unlikely that the revised picture of a socially diverse Enlightenment will be repainted. At the moment we can only conclude with Peter Gay that: 'Our information is too fragmentary and our statistics are too inconclusive to permit any generalisation except one: the consumers of the Enlightenment were distributed across educated society, unevenly but very widely' [107].

More informal but of major importance for the formation and diffusion of enlightened opinion were the salons of the capital.

Here more than anywhere was displayed the nobles' adoption of merit as the prime criterion of social value, as both noble and bourgeois intellectuals met to form one like-minded elite. It was a fusion given graphic expression by Lemonnier's justly celebrated painting of Madame de Geoffrin's salon, in which the intellectual elite of the day – Buffon, D'Alembert, Helvétius, Diderot, Montesquieu, Quesnay, Rousseau, Raynal, etc. – sit side by side with great aristocrats such as the Prince de Conti, the Duc de Nivernais, the Duchesse d'Anville and the Maréchal de Richelieu.

This was a relatively early development. From at least the 1730s, admission to the salons was being based more on merit than rank, and progressive nobles – Montesquieu, for example – were engaging freely in social and intellectual intercourse with commoners. It was a process assisted by an education common to the upper echelons of both nobles and bourgeois. In the increasingly meritocratic and competitive world of the eighteenth century, a good education was increasingly prized. As Chaussinand-Nogaret has pointed out:

> To have access to this education was not strictly a privilege of birth, but rather one of wealth. The rich middle classes also took advantage of it, and in the best schools the sons of tax-farmers rubbed shoulders with the sons of dukes and princes of the blood. In this way a cultural elite emerged in which old stock mingled with new blood and magistrates-to-be with officers-to-be [52].

Even if it is established, however, that the soil from which enlightened ideas grew was a mixture of sand and loam, it does not follow necessarily that those ideas lacked all social character. It is possible, at least, that for reasons of fashion and/or stupidity the nobles espoused ideas inimical to their interests. Two problems confront us here: determining the essential ideas of the Enlightenment, and determining the essential interests of the nobility. The first is the easier of the two. If the French Enlightenment was a broad enough church to include within its congregation members as different as Montesquieu and Rousseau, at least some sort of list of unitarian articles can be found. It seems reasonable to conclude, with Peter Gay, that the philosophes wanted a social and political order which would be secular, reasonable, humane, pacific, open and free – free in the sense of 'freedom from arbitrary power, freedom of speech, freedom of trade, freedom to realise one's talents, freedom of aesthetic response, freedom, in a word, of moral man to make his own way in the world' [105].

Conspicuous by its absence from this list is 'equal', for the philosophes were not egalitarian, but meritocratic. Even that should have made them hostile to privileges sanctioned only by birth, but – with a few exceptions – they proved to be remarkably tender towards aristocratic sensibilities. Although unequivocally hostile to such manifest abuses as the game laws, they did not call for the total abolition of the noble order to which so many of them belonged [115]. Real radicalism they reserved for revealed religion.

If it then be asked whether the Enlightenment was hostile to the interests of the nobility, the answer must be conditional on the nature of the noble in question. If he were an intolerant Catholic who set great store by inherited privilege and believed that all was for the best in this the best of all possible feudal worlds, then the new society envisaged by the philosophes was not for him. But if he were confident in his own abilities, and eager to employ them unimpeded by current restrictions, he had every reason to give it a warm welcome. It was a clash of cultures comparable to that depicted by Fielding in the persons of Squire Western and Mr Allworthy.

It is difficult to see the Enlightenment as unequivocally hostile to the old regime as a whole. The fundamental characteristics of the latter can be summarised as absolutist, Catholic, privileged, hierarchical, particularist (in the sense that loyalties beyond the local community were felt to a province or to the king rather than to an abstraction such as the nation) and agrarian [46]. Of course, only the second can be said to have been rejected axiomatically by the philosophes. Catholicism as an ideology was rejected for its irrationalism, the Catholic Church as an institution was rejected for its wealth, power, corruption and intolerance. Such *causes célèbres* as the Calas and the Chevalier de la Barre affairs periodically gave Voltaire's slogan *'écrasez l'infâme'* fresh urgency [106].

Yet in other departments, hostility was directed less towards the essence of the old regime than to its abuses. The only coherent economic theory developed by the French Enlightenment – by the physiocrats – was positively favourable towards agriculture and the land, deemed the only true source of wealth. Their political theories ranged from left to right, from the aristocratic constitutionalism of Montesquieu to the plebeian democracy of Rousseau: 'they all agreed about decency: they were for it. And they all agreed about religion: they were against it. But their political ideas and ideals covered a wide spectrum of possibilities' [107]. If few were as pragmatic as Voltaire, who managed to advocate almost every form of government, depending on which European state he was discussing at the time, no clear programme for political change inimical to the existing political system of France emerged.

In social terms, the story of the philosophes in the eighteenth century is the story of assimilation and integration, not alienation. Their progress is neatly symbolised by two contrasting vignettes: the thrashing Voltaire received in 1726 from the lackeys of the Chevalier de Rohan for poking fun at their master, and Voltaire's triumphant return to Paris in 1778 just before his death, when Parisian high society gathered to celebrate his apotheosis. During the intervening half-century, Voltaire and his colleagues had first infiltrated and then taken over the old regime's cultural institutions, including the Académie Française in 1772, which they turned into 'a sort of clubhouse' [102]. They had been aided and abetted by a growing number of sympathetic ministers and civil servants, who also ensured that the philosophes' material needs were met by the liberal distribution of pensions. By the late 1770s the philosophes had been comfortably assimilated into old regime society, as was demonstrated by Voltaire's apotheosis on his last visit to the capital in 1778.

The French Enlightenment was a movement *of* the educated elites *for* the educated elites. With the eternal exception of Rousseau, its most influential representatives did not believe the enlightenment of the masses to be either possible or desirable. Popular education should be confined to the 'three Rs' and a measure of physical, occupational and moral training, for its primary purpose was to promote economic utility and social stability, nothing more. In Voltaire's opinion: 'the enlightened times will only enlighten a small number of right-thinking people (*honnêtes gens*). The common people will always be fanatics' – by which he meant attached to religion. Voltaire, of course, was very much a member of the older generation of philosophes – he was born in 1694 – and by the time he made that remark (1759) was very much an establishment figure, but his patrician views were representative of later generations too. Baron Holbach, who lived to see the outbreak of the Revolution and is sometimes described as a democrat, was always careful to distinguish between property-owners and 'the imbecilic masses who, lacking all enlightenment and good sense, can become at any moment the tool and accomplice of subversive demagogues who seek to disrupt society' and demanded 'let us never protest against that inequality which has always been necessary'.

(iv)   The Public Sphere and Public Opinion

Views such as these did not prevent many contemporaries expressing the belief that the French Revolution was the result of a conspiracy hatched by the philosophes. As Edmund Burke observed in 1790 in his *Reflections on the Revolution in France*: 'I hear on all hands that a cabal, calling itself philosophic, receives the glory of many of the late proceedings; and that their opinions and systems are the true actuating spirit of the whole of them.' As the growing radicalism of the Revolution polarised European opinion into left and right, conspiracy theories mushroomed. If these paranoid fancies could not survive scholarly analysis, the notion that the Revolution must have had its origins in the Enlightenment proved to have a very long life ahead of it [117]. Recently, however, it has been challenged, not only on the grounds that the philosophes were anything but radical opponents of the old regime but also for methodological reasons. To assume that the Revolution was 'caused' by the Enlightenment just because it followed chronologically, it is argued, is to make the popular but fallacious assumption of *post hoc ergo propter hoc*, a notorious trap for the analyst in a hurry. Indeed, some bold spirits have turned the connection on its head, arguing that it was the Revolution which made the Enlightenment, not the other way round [96]. That is less perverse than it sounds, for once the revolutionaries had claimed the philosophes as their own, they ensured that we would view their apparent predecessors through a distorted lens.

Post-revisionist scholars have also rejected the very idea that the

French Revolution could have had intellectual origins [94]. Instead, they advance a cultural interpretation. If we are to understand what is distinctive about their approach and findings, then we need first to understand their vocabulary. In particular, we need to understand certain key words which are frequently used but rarely explained, especially 'culture', 'political culture' and 'discourse'. These look straightforward enough, having none of the unfamiliarity of other favourites among historians seeking a veneer of sophistication such as 'hermeneutics' or 'reification', but this turns out to be one linguistic area where common sense is not enough.

The most slippery but also the most important of these *'faux amis'* is 'culture'. This does not mean 'culture' in the commonly accepted sense, as in 'You can lead a whore to culture but you can't make her think' (Dorothy Parker) or 'When I hear the word "culture" I reach for my revolver' (Hermann Goering). This sense of 'culture' as painting, literature or music is of relatively recent origin, coming into general use only in the late nineteenth century. What the post-revisionist historians mean by 'culture' is the definition which derives from anthropology. Significantly, it was in the eighteenth century that it entered most European languages. First used as a synonym for 'civilisation' in general and as the antonym of 'barbarism', it was refined by the German theorist Johann Gottfried Herder (1744–1803) to apply to specific societies in specific places at specific times. Herder believed that every people (*Volk*) had its own customs, institutions, values and identity and that each was as valid as any other. So he also believed that every culture should be viewed sympathetically, from the inside and on its own terms.

We cannot follow the further development of the concept in any detail. It must suffice to say that by the late nineteenth century, 'culture' had acquired its modern anthropological meaning, best expressed by Sir Edward Tylor in *Primitive Culture* (1871) as 'that complex whole which includes knowledge, belief, art, morals, law, custom and any other capabilities and habits acquired by man as a member of society'. That would seem to be such a capacious category that it can accommodate almost anything. It acquires greater and more precise meaning when its autonomous status is established. The 'complex whole' known as culture is not determined by the material conditions of society, nor is it the superstructure which rises on the foundations provided by the economic forces of production, rather it enjoys its own independent existence. Of course it is influenced by such environmental forces as climate or geography but its dynamic is self-generated and it is 'self-referential', that is to say its component parts acquire meaning in relation to each other, not to some extraneous and allegedly more fundamental phenomenon. Of course, this places those who subscribe to this definition of culture at odds with Marxists who must view it as determined by class identity. Even such a sensitive and undogmatic Marxist as Raymond Williams insisted that economic structure must be seen as 'the guiding string on which culture is woven' [134].

Culture also acquires a firmer outline when the common currency which holds together its disparate ingredients is identified. This is language: 'Man is unique in that he alone possesses the ability to symbol, i.e. to bestow, freely and arbitrarily, meaning upon things and events, objects and acts. Articulate speech is the most characteristic and important form of symboling. All culture was produced and has been perpetuated by symboling in general and by articulate speech in particular' [133]. But just as any culture has a specific identity in space and time, so does its language. Words may be spelt the same way at different times and in different places, but they change their meaning according to who is saying what to whom, where, when and why. Language in this total context is termed 'discourse', as in 'the discourse of the old regime' or 'the discourse of the French Revolution'. To understand what is happening in a culture, therefore, it is not enough to read the main texts of the great thinkers; the whole 'ideological context' must be investigated [131].

This is particularly true of political culture. To suppose that the origins of the French Revolution can be found in a textual analysis of Diderot and D'Alembert's *Encyclopédie* or Rousseau's *Social Contract* reveals a woefully limited understanding of the political process. What is needed is an examination of the whole culture. Perhaps the best definition of this approach has been offered by Keith Michael Baker. 'The definition offered here [of political culture] is more linguistic. It sees politics as about making claims; as the activity through which individuals and groups in society articulate, negotiate, implement, and enforce the competing claims they make upon one another and upon the whole. Political

25

no longer received from the court; it no longer decides on reputations of any sort . . . The court's judgments are countermanded; one says openly that it understands nothing; it has no ideas on the subject [and] could have none . . . The court has thus lost the ascendancy that it had regarding the fine arts, literature, and everything pertaining to them today' [96]. This was more than the exchange of one gilded aristocratic frame for another, for both the size and nature of the Parisian audience was changing. Not only was the capital expanding rapidly in population, it was also becoming much more literate. The evidence may be fragmentary but it all points in the same direction – towards mass literacy. By 1789, 90 per cent of male Parisians and 80 per cent of females could sign their wills (although of course only owners of property made wills) and 66 per cent of men and 62 per cent of women surviving their marriage partners were able to sign the inventory of their inheritance. According to Mercier, 'ten times' more Parisians were reading in 1788 than a hundred years earlier. The result was the formation of a literary market to meet growing demand, the production of many more titles in much larger and cheaper editions and so a change in the *way* in which people read. Whereas in the past most of those who could read did so 'intensively', that is to say they read a few texts (mainly religious) again and again, now a growing number did so 'extensively', that is to say they read many more titles, often borrowing them from the lending libraries which proliferated, but only once.

The crucial consequence of this cultural diffusion was a sea-change in the criterion of cultural value. In the past it had been the royal academies which had decided what was good and to be encouraged and what was bad and to be suppressed. Increasingly it was now the consumers – the public – who pronounced the verdict. This was an early development and moreover one which affected all branches of the arts. The decision of the Royal Academy of Painting to resume its biennial public exhibitions in 1737, for example, was greeted by the *Mercure de France* in the following suggestive terms:

The Academy does well to render a sort of accounting to the public of its work and to make known the progress achieved in the arts it nurtures by bringing to light the work of its most distinguished members in the diverse genres it embraces, so that each thereby submits himself to the judgment of informed persons gathered in the greatest possible number and receives the praise or blame due to him [124].

Ten years later, La Font de Saint-Yenne (usually regarded as the first modern art critic) wrote in 1747: 'It is only in the mouths of those firm and equitable men who compose the Public, who have no links whatever with the artists . . . that we can find the language of truth.' The rise to pre-eminence of this new arbiter was repeated in other branches of the arts. During the '*querelle des bouffons*' over the relative merits of French and Italian music during the early 1750s, appeal was made by both sides to the public, 'because it alone has the right to decide whether a work will be preserved for posterity or will be used by grocers as wrapping-paper' and because the subjectivism of the individual in aesthetic matters can only be corrected 'by the verdict of the public, which is always governed by true feelings and rational opinions', as one pamphlet put it. There is also plenty of evidence that contemporaries made the connection between the right of the public to judge aesthetics and the right to judge politics. A very good example was supplied by D'Alembert in an essay published in 1759:

I am amazed that in a century when so many pens write about the liberty of commerce, the liberty of marriages, the liberty of the press, or the liberty of painting, no one has yet written about THE LIBERTY OF MUSIC . . . Our great statesmen reply: 'You are being short-sighted, for all liberties are interrelated and are all equally dangerous. The liberty of music assumes that of feeling, the liberty of feeling leads on to that of thinking, and the liberty of thinking to that of action, and the liberty of action is the ruination of states. So let us keep the opera as it is, if we wish to preserve the kingdom; and let us put a brake on the liberty of singing if we don't wish to see the liberty of talking following hard on its heels . . . It may be difficult to believe, but it is literally true that in the vocabulary of certain people, the work 'Bouffonist' [a supporter of Italian *opera buffa*], 'republican', 'rebel', 'atheist' (I almost forgot to add 'materialist') are pretty well synonymous.

Just when the public turned to expressing its 'true feelings and rational opinions' about politics is a matter for debate. It has been

29

argued that the process began much earlier than is usually thought and that Habermas' chronology is mistaken [95]. However, there seems little doubt that it was around mid-century that contemporaries began to perceive a change. In an address to the Académie Française delivered in 1787, Claude-Carloman de Rulhière dated the birth of public opinion to the years between the conclusion of the War of the Austrian Succession (1748) and the outbreak of the Seven Years War (1756). He also echoed the verdict of Mercier cited earlier that the capital had abandoned its deferential attitude to the court and 'it was then that there arose among us what we have called the empire of public opinion' [130]. Although he could not have known it when he spoke, it was also in 1749 that the Marquis d'Argenson anticipated his assessment by recording in his journal: 'Fifty years ago, members of the general public had no interest in political news, but today everyone reads his *Gazette de Paris*, even in the provinces. And although their opinions are quite misguided, they do take an interest in political matters.' Two years later he wrote with extraordinary prescience:

There is a philosophical wind blowing towards us from England in favour of free, anti-monarchical government; it is entering minds and one knows how opinion governs the world. It could be that this government is already accomplished in people's heads, to be implemented at the first chance; and the revolution might occur with less conflict than one thinks. All the orders of society are discontented together . . . a disturbance could turn into a revolt, and a revolt into a total revolution [96].

But why was this wind so 'anti-monarchical'? As the English example showed, there was no reason why the growth of public opinion in the public sphere should lead to violent revolution. On the contrary, the English monarchy was stronger in 1800 than it had been in 1700. Several explanations have been advanced, none of them mutually exclusive. The most cogent points to the *parlements* as the main agents in the discrediting of the monarchy. In 1713, as part of his campaign against religious dissent, Louis XIV had obtained from Rome a bull known as 'Unigenitus', which condemned the Jansenist movement for religious renewal within the Catholic Church as heretical. By thus permitting – indeed soliciting – foreign interference in the domestic affairs of his kingdom, he touched one of the most sensitive nerves in the French body politic. When his successors decided to continue the anti-Jansenist campaign, they also placed the monarchy at odds with what was perceived as national integrity. To the fore in organising opposition were the *parlements*, which on Louis XIV's death in 1715 regained their right to remonstrate before registering royal edicts. In a series of bruising disputes over the Jansenist issue in the 1730s and 1750s, they presented themselves as representatives of the national interest: 'The Parlement never speaks to the nation except in the name of the King, and equally it never speaks to the King except in the name of the nation' was how the Parlement of Rennes neatly put it in 1757. Increasingly, and with growing success, they sought to mobilise public opinion by publishing their remonstrances. Louis XV and his minister proved unable to compete in this new arena, veering from attempts at coercion to craven capitulation.

The monarchy sustained two terrible wounds in the course of this dispute. Firstly, its periodic attempts to strong-arm the *parlements* attracted accusations of 'despotism', *the* great term of abuse in eighteenth-century politics (comparable in its hateful associations with 'racism' today). In the past, French constitutional theorists had liked to draw a distinction between two forms of authoritarian government – 'absolutism' (good) and 'despotism' (bad) – but the mid-century disputes put paid to that. Now all forms of absolutist government were deemed illegitimate [78]. As William Doyle has written: 'Above all, despotism was a charge hurled with ever-increasing frequency at the government and its agents. By the 1780s it almost seemed as if government and despotism were synonyms in the public mind. And this suggests that the old order had lost the confidence of those who lived under it' [1]. Secondly, the monarchy allowed to slip from its grasp what was potentially its strongest card – its embodiment of national unity and the national interest. If the king could not defend national interests, indeed acted against them, then sovereignty would have to be sought elsewhere. It was found in the principle of 'national sovereignty' and for the time being at least, it was the *parlements* which had the best claim to be its depository. As J. S. Bromley wrote in an old but still important article: 'national sovereignty was the most dynamic concept that was crystallised out of the parliamentary struggle . . . parliamentary Jansenism, and with it what d'Argenson called Jansenist nationalism, did more to shake the fabric of French absolutism, in its theory and its practice, than the philosophers . . . perhaps they [*the parlements*] were the real educators of the *sans-culottes*' [77]. That verdict has been confirmed by one of the leading present-day historians of the *parlements*, Dale van Kley, who has identified the Jansenist disputes as 'major landmarks on a polemical road which gradually bifurcated toward both Revolution and counter-Revolution' [89].

Of all the milestones on that road, the most prominent was the 'Brittany affair' which began in November 1763 and reached a climax in January 1771 when Louis XV's chief minister, Maupeou, launched a *coup d'état* from above to deal with parlementary opposition once and for all. This protracted but fascinating dispute has been ably recounted and analysed elsewhere [87]; here we need only to identify the outcome. First and foremost, it confirmed the association of absolutism with despotism. On 3 March 1766 Louis XV went in person to the Parlement of Paris to issue a stinging reprimand. In what became aptly known as the *séance de la flagellation*, he made the following unequivocal statement on the personal and unlimited nature of his power:

It is in my person alone that sovereign authority resides . . . It is from me alone that my courts owe their existence and their authority. The plenitude of that authority, which they exercise only in my name, remains always in me, and can never be turned against me. It is to me alone that legislative power belongs without dependence and without any division . . . The whole public order derives from me, and the rights and interests of the nation . . . are necessarily joined with mine and rest only in my hands.

To most contemporaries, it seemed that the king was as despotic in action as he was in rhetoric, for he abused his power by interfering with the due process of the law, to persecute his opponents and to annul court action against his own agents. This reached a climax in January 1771 when the *parlements* were purged of dissidents and remodelled to allow royal control. Paradoxically, the chief danger for the monarchy lay in the fact that this exercise succeeded. Other more pliable judges were found to carry on the king's business and the troublesome *parlements* became a thing of the past. But the victory was illusory. Although stemming primarily from a (successful) manoeuvre to discredit the Duc de Choiseul [81], Maupeou's *coup d'état* caused a tremendous furore, inspiring a fierce, widespread and sustained debate about the political principles underlying the old regime. Although the government found some support (most notably from Voltaire), the majority of enlightened opinion, both noble and bourgeois, condemned its action as despotic. It was particularly ominous that a significant number of critics found neither royalist absolutism nor parlementary aristocracy attractive and looked forward to liberal constitutionalism. In the words of the episode's most recent historian, Durand Echeverria, it 'contributed to a profound and lasting transformation in the way in which the French thought about their government and their society' [83].

In other words, by the time Louis XVI came to the throne in 1774 the political system he had inherited had lost its legitimacy. On the one hand, public opinion had replaced the king as the source of authority, on the other hand the actions of Louis XV had given the monarchy an anti-national and despotic image. Unlike his near-contemporary, Frederick the Great (the self-styled 'first servant of the state'), Louis XV had failed to modernise the ideological foundations of his legitimacy by associating his person with an abstraction such as the state or nation and thus 'objectivising' his authority. As the Abbé de Veri commented: 'Today, hardly anyone dare say in Parisian society, I serve the king . . . You'd be taken for one of the chief valets at Versailles. *I serve the state* is the expression most commonly used'. The best summary of the new political culture which had emerged has been provided by Keith Michael Baker, the most cogent and influential of the post-revisionist historians:

> The political culture of absolutism had already been transformed in its last decades by changes that brought a new political space into existence well before 1789. If the press was the medium of this political space, 'public opinion' was its ultimate principle of authority . . . 'Public opinion' had become the articulating concept of a new political space with a legitimacy and authority apart from that of the crown: a public space in which the nation could reclaim its rights against the crown. Within this space, the French Revolution became thinkable [94].

But why was Louis XVI unable to repair the damage? Soon after his accession, he took the advice of his *de facto* chief minister, the Comte de Maurepas, dismissed Maupeou and restored the *parlements*. Suitably chastened, the latter made one or two angry noises to announce their return but then relapsed into relative quiescence for more than a decade. It would be tempting to argue that the political culture of the old regime had changed so profoundly by this stage that no amount of concessions could work the absolute monarchy's passage back into the goodwill of the nation. Only a systemic change would suffice. There is certainly something in this, but it may well be too determinist for most tastes.

One serious problem which Louis XVI might have solved if he had possessed greater resources of character and judgment was the factionalism of his court. The system created by Louis XIV at Versailles was designed to direct the energies and ambitions of his nobles away from conspiracy and towards an elaborate ritual designed to elevate the monarch. By supporting his personal charisma with hard work, Louis made it work remarkably well, setting a pattern of absolute kingship and representational culture which was imitated across Europe. Faltering even before 1715, it fell apart under his successor. Louis XV possessed certain assets which should have stood him in good stead as king of France: he was intelligent (the most intelligent of all the Bourbons according to his admiring biographer [73]), tall, strong, good-looking and virile. Alas, he was also timid, secretive, evasive, indecisive and cursed with a poor speaking voice. So he could not make Louis XIV's court-system operate. Increasingly he withdrew from the public life of the court into his private apartments or away from Versailles altogether to one of his smaller châteaux. In 1750, for example, he spent only 52 nights at Versailles [90]. But when he was away the court was dead and the courtiers moved back to Paris. His successor was equally lacking in the skills needed to make the court work. Although 'not a total cretin', as his brother-in-law Joseph II conceded grudgingly, he was also singularly unimpressive, perhaps his most damaging failing being his indecisiveness: 'trying to comprehend the king's ideas is like trying to hold on to greased billiard balls' was the unkind verdict of his brother, the Comte de Provence. The chronic indecision and consequent instability which afflicted the reigns of both Louis XV and Louis XVI enhanced the general sense of decay which hung about the monarchy. This was revealed by the increasingly rapid turnover of personnel in two of the most important offices of state: the secretary of state for war and the controller-general of finance. Between 1715 and 1789 there were 18 different secretaries of state for war; during a similar period in the previous century there had been just five. In the all-important department of finance, the situation was even more fluid: between 1715 and 1789 there were no fewer than 25 controllers-general of finance, giving an average life expectancy of rather less than three years. Here too, the pace of change was accelerating – 17 of those 25 served between 1754 and 1789, enjoying an average tenure of just over two years. During the last desperate 18 months of the old regime, six controllers-general were tried, so by then the average was down to just two and a half months!

Louis XVI proved no better than his grandfather in making the court work, taking refuge in hunting or in his workshop from the public life he hated. On only two occasions did he stir his ponderous hulk into leaving the Versailles–Paris region: in 1786 when he travelled to Cherbourg to inspect the new harbour installations – and in 1791 when he tried to run away from the Revolution. Symbolic of the musty, old-fashioned flavour of his kingship was the way in which he chose to be crowned. It was his personal decision to insist on the full sacramental panoply, including anointment with the sacred oil of Clovis (originally brought down from heaven by the Holy Ghost, or so it was believed). Going out of his way to dramatise the extent to which the clock was going back, he revived the ceremony of 'touching for the King's evil' (not performed since 1738), laying hands on 2,400 scrofulous invalids assembled specially in a park and thus claiming semi-divine status as *roi thaumaturge* [91, 93]. The contrast between pretension and reality left a yawning credibility gap: where once the Sun King had stood in all his awe-inspiring glory there was now a vacuum.

Into the vacuum moved the factions, seeking both political influence and patronage. There are good modern accounts of the politics of the Versailles court in its dying years [84, 86], so only the broadest of outlines is needed here. Essentially, the court divided between a 'King's Party', which championed the traditional values of royal authority, orthodox Catholicism and the old system of foreign alliances, and a 'Queen's Party', which was sympathetic to the *parlements*, had close links with the philosophes and supported the Austrian alliance. As the name suggests, the latter was centred on Marie Antoinette, who used her strong personality and physical attraction to exert an influence on Louis XVI which was never total but was always injurious: 'the crucial ingredient in the reign of Louis XVI was the personal ascendancy of Marie Antoinette . . . The split between the king's ministers and the queen brought about by this situation cannot be overestimated as a cause of the ultimate fall of the monarchy' [86]. Courts have always had their factions; what made the situation in the 1770s and 1780s so dangerous was Louis XVI's inability to bang heads together and force them in a single direction. Experience had shown again and again that an absolute monarchy could be ruled effectively only if the king took charge himself (Louis XIV) or delegated his authority to a first minister (Richelieu). Louis XVI did neither. Although Maurepas never enjoyed the title or substance of first minister, at least he had provided some sort of cohesion, but when he died in 1781 what was already a soft centre began to implode.

To make matters worse, the political cost of this dereliction was intensified by a public campaign of vilification directed at the sexual life of the royal family. This had begun in the previous reign when Louis XV's notorious libertinism was both advertised and greatly exaggerated in a wave of political pornography [75]. The immorality of Bourbon monarchs was legendary of course, but whereas Louis XIV had been presented as a virile gallant, flaunting the potency which made him the rightful head of the herd, the Louis XV pictured in the *libelles* was a seedy decadent, seeking to revive his flagging powers with common prostitutes. That his last official mistress – Madame du Barry – had indeed been a courtesan lent credence to these stories. That his successor's conduct was unimpeachable did nothing to turn the tide. On the contrary, the fact that Louis XVI was able to consummate his marriage only seven years after the event injected a further and probably fatal ingredient into the unsavoury stew – contempt. It also switched attention to his consort.

When Marie Antoinette arrived in France in 1770 to marry the dauphin, she was young (fifteen), tall, blonde and beautiful. She was also headstrong, fun-loving, self-centred and stupid. It was a combination certain to attract the attention of the *libellistes*, the ancestors of tabloid journalists. If she could not help one cause of her unpopularity – her Austrian birth – she could certainly have been more prudent in her behaviour at court. By gathering around her a favoured few, by exploiting her hold on her husband to make and unmake appointments, and by indulging in reckless extravagance, she provided the gossipmongers with an *embarras de richesses*. Among many other things, it was alleged that Louis XVI was not the father of the children she eventually bore him; that she was wildly promiscuous, her lovers including her brother-in-law, the Comte d'Artois; that she had infected the court with venereal disease; and that she engaged in lesbian orgies with her close friends the Princesse de Lamballe and the Duchesse de Polignac [101]. Steadily gathering momentum between 1774 and 1788, political pornography really took off after 1789, with the queen as the central target. Typical of many pamphlets was *L'Autrichienne en goguettes* ['The Austrian bitch on the spree'] in which Louis XVI passes out after drinking too much champagne, allowing Marie Antoinette to engage in an obscene threesome with the Duchesse de Polignac and the Comte d'Artois [156].

The strong element of sexual psychopathology which surfaced time and again during the course of the Revolution suggests that this socio-political pornography made a deep impression on the revolutionary crowd's image of the privileged orders and, in particular, of the royal family. When, for example, the Princesse de Lamballe, one of the queen's alleged lovers, was butchered during the September Massacres of 1792, a crowd set out for the Temple prison bearing her head on a pike, dragging her body behind and with her bowels carried separately, chanting that Marie Antoinette should be made to kiss the lips of her whore. This reputation for depravity pursued her to the end. At her trial in October 1793, Marie Antoinette was accused not only of treason but also of committing incest with her eight-year-old son and at her public execution the latest *libelles* were on sale, including *Les Adieux de la Reine à ses mignons et mignonnes*.

How much impact this torrent of filth had on the fate of the monarchy is difficult to assess. An emphatic view has come from the historian who has made this dark corner very much his own – Robert Darnton. During the past twenty-five years he has constantly repeated his belief that the really corrosive force gnawing away at the foundations of the old regime was not the 'High Enlightenment', represented by Montesquieu, Voltaire, Diderot and company, but the gutter press of the *libellistes*. As the eighteenth century progressed, he states, the philosophes had lost their cutting edge and had been absorbed into the establishment: 'By 1778, when all of Paris was salaaming before Voltaire, the last generation of philosophes had become pensioned, petted and completely integrated in high society' [98]. The *libellistes*, on the other hand, were angry young men who had come to Paris to make their fortunes, had failed to break into the charmed circles of the High Enlightenment and so vented their frustration in truly radical attacks on the establishment [102]. Although of course banned, the *libelles* in fact circulated freely, especially in Paris, allowing their poison to sink deep into the roots of the old regime. Darnton concludes: 'Forbidden books moulded public opinion in two ways: by fixing disaffection in print (preserving and spreading the word), and by fitting it into narratives (transforming loose talk into coherent discourse)' [99].

The fluency of Darnton's writing, together with the titillating nature of his material, have given his interpretation wide currency and a long life. There are now increasing signs, however, of a reaction. In particular, it has been argued, his contempt for what he calls 'the great-man, great-book variety of literary history' [101] has made him blind to what really eroded the old regime's legitimacy. Just as, *pace* Bentham, pushpin is *not* as good as poetry, Voltaire or Diderot *were* more destructive than Darnton's anonymous pornographers. It has been pointed out that to recognise the importance of the philosophes does not necessarily involve a return to the 'ideas without people' approach of old-fashioned intellectual historians. In Sarah Maza's judicious assessment: 'we need not necessarily throw out the baby of Great Works along with the bathwater of teleological distortion. But only if we trace the connections between canonical texts and lesser-known works will we be able to reconstitute the linguistic and broader cultural contexts within which the Revolution became "thinkable"' [128]. It has also been suggested that Darnton has exaggerated the contrast between the allegedly integrated philosophes and the allegedly alienated *libellistes* [110]. Voltaire or Diderot certainly never saw themselves as part of any establishment. Together with all the other philosophes, 'high' and 'low', they suffered throughout their careers from government censorship. Here, as so often, the regime contrived to have the worst of both worlds. On the one hand, the ever-growing army of censors (76 in 1741, 178 by 1789) and ever-multiplying censorship regulations (1757, 1764, 1767, 1783, 1785) made life difficult and even dangerous for any author straying beyond the narrow limits of orthodox ideology. Many philosophes (including Diderot and Voltaire) spent time in prison, all of them lived under its shadow. On the other hand, the attempt at repression was woefully inefficient. Sabotaged from within – by courtiers such as Madame de Pompadour, no less, and ministers such as Malesherbes, who intervened to protect the philosophes – it only served to stimulate appetites for illicit literature. When Morellet was sent to the Bastille after falling foul of the censors, his friends consoled him by pointing out that imprisonment would make his fortune [117].

So, however much the philosophes may have been assimilated into high *society*, they necessarily remained alienated from *government*. They took its pensions but remained on the outside, looking in – with an increasingly critical eye. Although Louis XVI's ministers did in fact initiate important reform programmes [10], they failed to persuade public opinion that this was a regime moving with the times towards liberal constitutionalism and modernity. In short, the monarchy had a serious 'image problem', appearing both weak and oppressive. The point has been well made by Norman Hampson in an illuminating comparison of Burke and Montesquieu and of Dr Johnson and Voltaire. In terms of actual ideas and attitudes, little divided one from the other. What made the Frenchmen so much more hostile to their regime was the fact that they were forced to see themselves 'as a kind of perpetual opposition, with the tendency towards generalised and abstract criticism that the role usually implies' [111].

On the other hand, radical journalists such as Brissot or Marat would have been horrified to find themselves classed as part of a literary proletariat. The latter group did not vilify the representative figures of the 'High Enlightenment' when they entered into their kingdom after 1789, on the contrary, they heaped them with praise and organised their formal apotheosis [110]. The nature of the illicit book trade has also been misrepresented. In the judgment of John Lough, it is nothing less than a 'wild exaggeration' to equate all clandestine publications with sedition. In fact the truly subversive publications constituted only a 'small minority' of the titles smuggled in, most being quite innocuous reprints of works already published quite legally in France [116].

Louis XVI's well-advertised shortcomings as a husband no doubt tarnished his image and made it easier for contemptuous members of the court to abandon the royal cause when the terminal crisis of the absolute monarchy began at the end of the 1780s. Yet on many occasions during the early stages of the Revolution he still proved capable of inspiring fervent demonstrations of loyalty from both legislators and general public, as spontaneous as they were patently sincere. On 14 December 1791, for example, he went to the National Assembly to announce that he had ordered the German princes to disperse the counter-revolutionary *émigrés* in their territories, to give a pledge to uphold the new revolutionary constitution and to make a ringing appeal for future cooperation to show that the king and nation were united. This unleashed a great wave of enthusiasm, recorded by the secretary of the Assembly as follows: 'The applause lasted for several minutes. From several members the shout resounded through the Assembly: Long live the King of the French! This shout was repeated by the public galleries and the large number of citizens who had found their way into the chamber in the wake of the King' [142].

This episode is revealing. Here the king stood forth as the defender of the national interest against foreign intervention and at once struck a deeply resonant chord in his audience. In doing so, he was performing the first of the two essential functions of the monarch. With very few exceptions, historians of the origins of the Revolution have concentrated exclusively on the other attribute of kingship – the maintenance of law – and how it was eroded in theory and practice. This historiographical oversight is no more excusable for being easy to understand. The marginalisation of France as a great power in the twentieth century, made only more obvious by periodic Gaullist attempts to tell the tide to turn, has put domestic concerns at the head of historians' agendas and has influenced their reading of the past. The French political nation of the late eighteenth century had a different perspective. They believed that France was potentially the greatest power on earth, by virtue of its wealth, population, location and history. Indeed, it had been just that in the recent past, under Louis XIV, 'when not a dog barked in Europe without the leave of the King of France'.

But how things had changed since those glory days! With the advantage of hindsight, we can see that the hegemony France briefly enjoyed in the last quarter of the seventeenth century was bound to be short-lived. As the rest of Europe caught up and as the British opened up a second front overseas, French resources became relatively smaller but had to be stretched much further. Most contemporaries were not inclined to take this structural view and, when French power began to wilt, preferred to look for human culprits and specific actions to blame. Top of their list was the 'diplomatic revolution' brought about by the Treaty of Versailles of 1 May 1756, when France abandoned nearly three centuries of hostility to the house of Habsburg and allied with Austria. So sudden and so drastic was this change that only immediate and dazzling success could have made it palatable. In the event, it was followed by catastrophe, as in the Seven Years War which followed, France was defeated by the British overseas and by the Prussians in Europe.

This was a truly world-historical moment, when among other things the decision was taken that eventually English would become the world's language. It was also the moment when the French absolute monarchy was stripped of a major part of its legitimacy. It was not so much that Louis XV had failed to defend his country's position in the world – even Louis XIV had lost wars – it was rather that he had created an alliance system which was perceived to be against the national interest. That Madame de Pompadour was believed to have played a major role in its creation only served to make it seem the more disgraceful. Far from cutting his losses after 1763, Louis XV maintained the alliance through thick and thin. It was to secure its long-term future that he married his heir to the Austrian archduchess Marie Antoinette in 1770 and it was the fact that she personified the hated relationship that accounted for much of her unpopularity. Not only was she accused of sexual excess, it was also claimed that she was acting as Joseph II's agent at Versailles (which was true) and was diverting huge amounts of French gold to her brother's coffers (which was not true).

After 1763 the French monarchy was spared such military humiliations as the battle of Rossbach on 5 November 1757, when Frederick the Great and 22,000 men had routed a French force twice that size in half an hour, but there were constant diplomatic reminders of how low France had come in the world. The brutal partition of Poland, one of France's oldest allies, in 1772 by the three eastern powers was deeply shaming, especially given the involvement of her supposed ally, Austria. Victory over the British in America after 1778 was spoilt by the failures of the last year of the war, which obliged French negotiators to accept much less than had been expected. The Russian annexation of the Crimea in 1783, Frederick the Great's formation of the League of Princes in 1785 and, above all, the failure to prevent the Prussians invading the Dutch Republic in 1787 all helped to confirm that France had ceased to be a great power [143]. In an age when the state did relatively little at home and so much more importance was attached to foreign policy, these failures cut very deep. From the rich range of similar verdicts available, the following observation by the Comte de Ségur is representative:

> Thus soon [after the Austrian alliance of 1756] the government no longer possessed any dignity, the finances any order and the conduct of policy any consistency. France lost its influence in Europe; England ruled the seas effortlessly and conquered the Indies unopposed. The powers of the North partitioned Poland. The balance of power established by the Peace of Westphalia was broken. The French monarchy ceased to be a first-rank power.

As we shall see, the disaffection this sense of degradation aroused in the officer corps of the royal army was to prove decisive when the final crisis erupted. Not for the first or last time, the similarities between events in France before 1789 and Russia before 1917 is very striking.

2 Impact: the Revolution

(i)   The Crisis of 1786–9

By themselves, neither the philosophes of the High Enlightenment nor the muck-rakers of Grub Street could have toppled the old regime. Once the regime had begun to totter for other reasons, however, they did get the chance to make their presence felt. It came at the end of the 1780s. On 20 August 1786 the luckless controller-general of finances of the day, Calonne, went to tell Louis XVI that the financial situation was critical. There was an annual deficit of about a hundred million livres on a total revenue of just 475 million; the third vingtième, established with considerable difficulty in 1782, was due to expire in 1787; 1,250 million livres had been borrowed since 1776 and it had become very difficult to raise more, even at prohibitive rates of interest. Only radical reform could stave off total collapse [135].

Thus began a sequence of events which led to the meeting of the Estates General at Versailles on 5 May 1789: the fiscal history of the *Ancien Régime* led directly to the Revolution [45]. What occurred during the intervening three years has been described in many accounts and there is no need to add to the list here. What does concern us is the social character of the terminal phase of the old regime and, in particular, the part played in it by the bourgeoisie.

The traditional interpretation finds the essence of the crisis in the old contradiction between the reforms the monarchy needed for its survival and the interests of the privileged orders on which it depended. The latter were simply irreconcilable with the former, so 'every time a reforming minister wanted to modernise the State, the aristocracy rose in defence of its privileges' (Albert Soboul) [24]. But this time the crown's financial problems were so serious, in the aftermath of the American war, that it had to persevere. That only served to provoke a reaction from the aristocracy even stronger than usual, a full-blooded revolt indeed, which opened the way for the bourgeoisie to move in like infantry behind tanks and to turn a squabble among feudal elites into a revolution.

There is something to be said for this scheme, but not everything. At least three important qualifications need to be made. In the first place, there was no simple confrontation between would-be modernising monarchy and reactionary privileged orders. As Jean Égret has shown, the Assembly of Notables – summoned in February 1787 to discuss the reforms proposed by Calonne – was not dominated by diehard defenders of the status quo. There was general agreement that fiscal privileges should be abolished, for example. Where they differed from the king and his advisers was over method. Far from seeking to create a more efficient and more soundly based royal absolutism, the Notables intended to make the most of this golden opportunity to dismantle it. So they made their co-operation conditional on a guarantee that there would be no return to the old mixture of despotism and incompetence [135]. Their dogged resistance, which led to the dismissal of Calonne in April 1787, was not a reactionary move; in the neat formulation of Denis Richet: 'The fall of Calonne was the fall of authoritarian reformism. The hour of liberalism had come'. It should be noted that Marie Antoinette played an important role in the disgrace of Calonne and the appointment of her protégé, Brienne. As one of the latter's first and worst decisions was to veto intervention against Prussia in the Dutch Republic, it proved to be catastrophic interference. Even she herself later recognised it to have been a terrible mistake [84].

It was the same liberal determination not to let the absolute monarchy off the hook until permanent *structural* reforms had been conceded that led to the trials and tribulations of Calonne's successor, Brienne, at the hands of the *parlements*. Of course it is impossible to be sure when ascribing motives, but it seems clear that when the *parlements* called for the convocation of the Estates General or proclaimed that the right to consent to taxation was a fundamental law of the kingdom, they were not just defending narrow class-interests but were also advancing principles which they believed to be essential to the national interest.

Needless to say, not all French nobles and clergy marched around in one great Gladstonian army of earnest liberals. There were enough reactionaries among them of the 'never-give-aninch' variety to give some semblance of reality to the sort of aristocrat who appears in Jacobin rhetoric, Charles Dickens' *A Tale of Two Cities* and Albert Soboul's *History of the French Revolution*. Even so, the number of nobles in the vanguard of radical agitation during this period is very striking. During the winter of 1788–9 a group known as the 'Society of Thirty' met regularly to co-ordinate the opposition's campaign in the elections to the Estates General. Its leaders were almost all nobles – among them, the Duc d'Aiguillon, the Duc de la Rochefoucauld, the Duc de Lauzun, the Marquis de Lafayette, the Marquis de Condorcet, the three Comtes de Lameth, the Comte de Mirabeau and the Vicomte de Noailles. Of the fifty-five members whose identity has been established, only five were commoners [139].

A further – and very important – qualification has to be made about the nature of noble aspirations in 1789, as revealed by the *cahiers de doléances*, the remonstrances drawn up nation-wide in each *bailliage* for consideration by the Estates General. A crucial issue was whether voting at the latter should be by order (which would have given a built-in majority to the clergy and nobility) or by head (which would have done the same for the Third Estate). Far from forming a united bloc against the Third Estate, the nobility divided. Only 41.04 per cent of the *cahiers* supported mandatory voting by order, results achieved often only after fierce debate and by small majorities. That figure was almost matched by the 38.76 per cent of the *cahiers* which actively supported or at least were prepared to accept voting by head. The remaining *cahiers* opted for voting by order, but did not make it an inflexible principle, or were selective (demanding voting by order for certain issues, by head for others) [52].

Even more striking was the coincidence of the views of the nobility and the Third Estate on how France should be reformed. Taking a representative sample of liberal demands, Table 1 shows that, if anything, the nobles were *more* liberal than their bourgeois colleagues. Certainly it is impossible to infer any confrontation between two diametrically opposed classes. This sort of table provides the revisionists with their best evidence of the pre-revolutionary fusion between noble and non-noble elites. It makes clear that both groups wanted the same solution to the country's problems: a moderate, peaceful change to a modernised constitutional monarchy, for their mutual benefit [30].

Table 1
Liberal Nobles in 1789

Cahiers de doléances which supported:	of the nobility %	of the 3rd estate %
Equality before the law	23	17
Abolition of *lettres de cachet*	68.65	74
Abolition of interference in the judicial procedure by the government	47	40
Introduction of Habeas Corpus	40	31
Giving accused legal representation	24	35
Insistence on the establishment of a constitution as a precondition of any further grant of taxation	64	57
Division of legislative power between the king and the Estates General	52	36
Giving legislative power to the Estates General only	14	20
Regular meetings of the Estates General	90	84
Parliamentary immunity	24	16
Control of taxation to the Estates General	81	82
Fiscal equality	88	86
Ministerial responsibility to the Estates General	73	74
A constitutional regime in general	62	49
Liberty of the Press	88	74
Freedom of commerce	35	42
Abolition of monoplies	59	72
More economic freedom in general	45	66
Abolition of seigneurial rights	14	64

[30, 52]

What is more, these liberal words of the nobles were supported by action. As was pointed out earlier, it was nobles who played the leading part in the Society of Thirty during the winter of 1788–9. It was also nobles who played the leading part once the Estates General had met. About ninety noble deputies, a third of the total, can be classified as liberal, and to them should be added several more sitting in the other two Estates. They quickly made their mark: it was the Comte de Mirabeau who emerged as the leader of the National Assembly (which the Estates General became at the end of June 1789), it was the Marquis de Lafayette who became the first commander of the Paris National Guard, it was the Vicomte de Noailles who introduced the decrees abolishing 'feudalism' on 4 August 1789, it was Talleyrand (a bishop as well as a noble) who proposed the secularisation of church land, it was the Comtes de Lameth who helped to found the Jacobin Club, and so on and so forth.

All this is well known. What is more often overlooked is the crucial role played by nobles in the collapse of the monarchy's last line of defence – the army. Demoralised by the catastrophes of the Seven Years War, disaffected with a foreign policy at odds with what they conceived to be the national interest, exasperated by the constant chopping and changing of military regulations, bitterly resenting the venal system which allowed wealthy young men to buy their way up the promotion ladder, the officer corps was in a thoroughly alienated frame of mind by the late 1780s [140].

They were made positively mutinous by yet another attempt to revamp the system beginning in 1787, under the direction of the Comte de Guibert, the most unpopular man in the French army. To the fore in the demonstrative sabotage of this exercise were men like the Lameth brothers, Lafayette and Lauzun, soon to make their mark as revolutionary politicians. Indeed, it is striking just how many liberal nobles were also army officers: in addition to the names just listed, there were Clermont-Tonnerre, La Rochefoucauld-Liancourt, La Rochefoucauld-Enville, Noailles, Aiguillon, Dillon, Mirabeau, and many more [79]. So when the king tried to use his army to suppress disorder in 1788–9, too many officers were too unreliable for his attempt at coercion to succeed. As Lafayette observed, it was the officers 'who gave their soldiers the first lessons in insubordination' [79]. When it is also recalled that more than three-quarters of the noble deputies at

Versailles – 221 out of 278 – were army officers and that eleven more noble officers sat with the Third Estate, it could be argued that the French Revolution was in part a military putsch. As Antoine Rivarol observed: 'the defection of the army is not one of the causes of the Revolution, it is the Revolution itself' [79].

If the nobility and the upper echelons of the bourgeoisie were so united in their wish to see a moderate and peaceful transformation of the old regime, it must now be asked why the leaders of the Third Estate employed such hostile language against the nobility and how it was possible for Mallet du Pan, for example, to make the often-quoted remark early in 1789: 'The public debate has changed. Now the King, despotism, the constitution are merely secondary: it is a war between the Third Estate and the other two orders'. The answer lies in the conflict created by the decision of the Parlement of Paris that the Estates General should meet in the form current when it last convened – in 1614. This led to many nobles of recent origin – the *anoblis* – being depressed into the Third Estate, and bitterly resenting the fact [36]. It also led the liberal nobles of the Society of Thirty to agitate for abolition of the 'forms of 1614', a campaign which proved counter-productive, for it only served to provoke the more conservative members of the privileged orders to take up entrenched positions under the banner of 'no concessions' [1]. It was an artificial conflict which was thus created, not a true conflict of interest, but it was to be many years before the rift could be healed and the noble-bourgeois elite reassembled in the shape of the post-revolutionary notables.

The delay was occasioned by the same force which made the Revolution so radical and so violent. It was the sudden eruption on to the national scene of the masses. Although their grievances were social and economic in character, their campaign to secure redress was to have profound political consequences. Its manifold long- and short-term origins have been examined in great detail by scores of scholars, and here only the briefest of outlines can be given.

If the single most important cause of the socio-economic crisis of the old regime has to be identified, then population pressure has the best credentials. The growth rate in the eighteenth century of rather less than 30 per cent was actually rather modest by contemporary standards (Great Britain's figure, for example, was more than double that) but France was, relatively speaking, a densely populated country even before the eighteenth-century increase began [61]. While there was still waste land to be put under the plough, while the harvests remained good, while the commercial and manufacturing sector remained buoyant – as was generally the case during the middle decades of the century, despite occasional hiccoughs – the surplus could be absorbed without too much difficulty. Even so, the trend was towards pauperisation, as both the number and proportion of peasants with midget plots or no land at all constantly grew. For everyone unable to grow all the food he and his family required – for the great majority, in other words – the standard of living was deteriorating, for the law of supply and demand sent up the price of food at the same time as it depressed the reward for labour: between the 1730s and 1789 prices increased three times faster than wages.

This secular trend was intensified from the late 1770s by a recession which affected all sectors of the economy except colonial trade. It had been a difficult decade altogether, with a subsistence crisis sparking off the 'flour war' in 1775, the most serious peasant rising before the Revolution. But it was the collapse of wine prices three years later, due to over-production and over-abundant harvests, which heralded a period of prolonged misery for the peasantry. Wine was so important a cash crop for so many peasants that this disaster had serious repercussions for the rest of the economy.

In the mid-1780s this enduring problem was intensified by bad weather which variously decimated forage crops together with the animals which depended on them, and ravaged industrial crops together with the manufacturers who depended on them. In this pre-industrial economy the interaction between the dominant agricultural sector and manufacturing was automatic and swift. A sudden increase in the price of food brought an equally sudden collapse in the demand for manufactured goods; that led necessarily to an equally sharp contraction in the demand for labour – just at a time when both peasants and urban labourers needed employment more than ever to cope with the higher prices. It was only those lucky peasants able to grow more than they needed for survival who flourished in such conditions – but they were in a small minority. As if this were not enough, there were some special problems afflicting the economy in the late 1780s, among them the Eden Treaty of 1786 which exposed French markets to British competition, a damaging trade dispute with Spain, and the war in the Baltic between Russia and Sweden which shut off the granaries of Prussia and Poland just when they were needed most.

Contemporaries were convinced that poverty and its associated problems were getting worse in the 1780s and all the evidence suggests that they were right. The most visible and alarming sign was the galloping expansion of groups on the margin of society, of foundlings, prostitutes, beggars, vagrants and criminals. Gangs of bandits more numerous, larger and more violent than anything seen in the past, terrorised the countryside with highway-robbery, burglary and extortion [64]. In the Parisian basin the problem was especially acute, for the large numbers of seasonal migrant labourers could change so easily from day labourers into beggars and criminals in times of crisis [144].

So it was an old regime both debilitated by deprivation and accustomed to social violence that the final disaster struck in the summer of 1788. In twenty-seven of thirty-two généralités the harvest failed, thus creating a subsistence crisis of unprecedented scope and severity. The result was that prices began to rise just when they should have been coming down and went on rising throughout the autumn and winter of 1788–9. It has been estimated that a working man in Paris could keep his family above the breadline only if the price of bread kept below two sous a pound; by July 1789 it had reached four sous a pound [17]. Perhaps even more inflammatory was the commonly held belief in a *pacte de famine*, a monstrous conspiracy by government and grain-dealers to make their fortunes at the expense of the people.

The news that the Estates General were to meet, the agitation surrounding the election of deputies and the discussion of grievances to be included in the *cahiers* all helped to raise the temperature even higher. All over France, both urban and rural violence increased, reaching a climax in July 1789 with the 'Great Fear' in the countryside and the storming of the Bastille at Paris. It was at this point that the catastrophic consequences of the unreliability of the army made their full impact. If Louis XVI had been able to disperse the Estates General (or the 'National Assembly', as it styled itself after 17 June 1789) and to restore order in Paris, he might well have been able to prevent what turned out to be the fatal fusion of the political crisis with the socio-economic crisis. Of course a coercive exercise could not have solved the financial problems of the monarchy but it would have won a vital breathing-space, for once the new harvest had been brought in, the social temperature would have dropped.

That is speculation. In the event, the 17,000-odd troops which could be moved from the frontier (characteristically, they were in the wrong place at the wrong time) only made matters worse. On the one hand, news of their assembly sent the temperature past boiling-point; on the other, they could not be used for fear that they would mutiny [136]. When the revolutionary crowd attacked the Bastille, they were not seeking to liberate political prisoners or to destroy a symbol of the old regime, they were looking for arms and ammunition with which to equip their new para-military force – the National Guard. That is the true importance of 14 July 1789 – it marked the collapse of the regime's most valuable asset: its monopoly of disciplined armed force. Once that monopoly had been broken, the Revolution had come to stay [143].

(ii)   The Revolution and the New Order

'By their fruits ye shall know them' (Matthew, vii. 20): on the face of it, an obvious test for the identification of the social character of the French Revolution would be an analysis of what the revolutionaries did when they came to power. That, surely, would shed light on the nature of their grievances and aspirations under the old regime. Unfortunately, it seems clear – to revisionist historians, at least – that the ideology of the revolutionaries was actually forged during the revolutionary crisis itself and that a sharp break occurred in 1789. The evidence of the *cahiers de doléances* suggests that the Enlightenment had not created a revolutionary mentality, that most people wanted moderate reform and that very few had any idea just how radical the Revolution would turn out to be. As George Taylor has argued: 'the revolutionary state of mind expressed in the Declaration of the Rights of Man and the decrees of 1789–91 was a product – and not a cause – of a crisis that began in 1787' [137]. In short, it was not the revolutionaries who made the Revolution but the Revolution which made the revolutionaries [1].

51

Nevertheless, even if it was the case, in the words of François Furet, that 'the revolutionary event, *from the very outset*, totally transformed the existing situation and created a new mode of historical action that was not intrinsically a part of that situation' [35], it is both legitimate and necessary to look at what the Revolution actually did. As soon as one does, one cannot help but be struck by the extent to which it furthered the interests of the bourgeois. At both a national and a local level it was they who benefited most from the new political arrangements. The electorate was divided into three – 'passive citizens', 'active citizens' and 'eligible electors' – on a sliding scale of wealth which in effect gave political power to the prosperous. Theoretically, a simple material criterion should have favoured nobles just as much, but in practice they dropped out of sight in the political life of most of the eighty-three departments into which France was now divided [12]. The great number of regional studies, which in most respects have stressed the heterogeneity of revolutionary France, have confirmed in detail that in one community after another it was the bourgeois who took control. This was not a fixed group, of course. On the contrary, the new men were in turn replaced by newer men, with the result that a large number acquired some kind of direct political experience in the course of the 1790s [154].

This new political class can be defined as 'bourgeois' in a loosely Marxist sense, both in terms of social position and class consciousness. Although various in terms of economic function, its members did own the means of production, whether in the form of capital, skills, tools or land. Although various in terms of political opinion, its members did unite in their rejection of feudalism, aristocracy and absolutism. Unfortunately, to use 'bourgeois' in this way does not take us very far. Such a capacious category cannot distinguish between militant republicans and moderate royalists. Neither can it accommodate the awkward fact that the most advanced parts of France, economically speaking, were often right-wing, while radical republicanism was most intense in the least capitalist regions [154].

Nevertheless, the social and economic policies of the National Assembly were also manifestly favourable to the bourgeoisie. In the meritocratic society they created, it was men of means and education who enjoyed a head start. The revolutionaries may have used universalistic rhetoric – may even have believed that they were acting in the interests of all – but it was clear who stood to benefit most. Even the Declaration of the Rights of Man and the Citizen, the most self-consciously universalist of all the revolutionary documents, declared private property to be a natural and inalienable right (a principle of little relevance to the great majority of Frenchmen who owned no property and had no prospect of doing so) [24]. The abolition of internal customs barriers, the abolition of privileged trading monopolies, the introduction of a uniform system of weights and measures, the method adopted for the sale of the *biens nationaux*, the Allarde law which abolished guilds, and the Le Chapelier law which outlawed workers' associations, all promoted bourgeois interests. On a more symbolic level, the abolition of noble titles and such honorific noble privileges as the right to bear arms and to sport heraldic devices, the introduction of 'citizen' as the approved form of address, and many more changes of the same stamp combined to elevate the bourgeoisie's social status.

But did these changes promote *only* bourgeois interests? Were not the enterprising nobles equally – or even additionally – favoured by the dismantling of the old regime's restrictions? The nobles were also men of means and education, indeed men of more means and better education than most of their bourgeois competitors. In exchange for abandoning a number of honorific privileges, to which many of them attached no importance anyway, they were now offered limitless opportunities for political and material advancement. Of course many nobles regarded the Revolution as the devil's work and could not even bring themselves to live in France while it lasted, but for every Comte d'Artois who demonstratively emigrated, there were a dozen who stayed at home and quietly got on with making the best of it. Only between 7 and 8 per cent of French nobles emigrated and not even all of them can be classified as unequivocally reactionary [151].

Attention is usually drawn to the number of nobles who emigrated, but more striking is the number of nobles who gave their active support to the Revolution, even during its most terrorist phase. The experience of the officer corps, the body most self-consciously devoted to old-regime values, is instructive, It is certainly the case that about 60 per cent of the officers had emigrated by the time war broke out – but what is more impressive is the fact that 3,000 remained. The revolutionary armies which gained the first great victories and conquests in 1792 were commanded by former nobles: Dumouriez, Montesquiou and Custine [136]. Despite repeated purges, there were still 900 noble officers serving in September 1793, a figure which was depleted during the Terror of year II (1793–4) but which rose again in 1795 to over a thousand, a hundred of whom were generals [151].

In the civilian sphere too, the degree of continuity is striking. Of the fifty-eight presidents elected by the Constituent Assembly, thirty-one were nobles [30]. And if noble representation was appreciably smaller in subsequent legislatures, it was still there. Even after the abolition of the monarchy, there were still forty nobles in the National Convention, many of them very radical and many of them leading lights (Condorcet, Kersaint, Barras, Hérault de Séchelles, Soubrany, Le Peletier de Saint-Fargeau [151]. One can even call on the experience of *counter*-revolutionaries to show how tenacious was noble support for the Revolution. The Comte de Puisaye, for example, the leading counter-revolutionary commander in the West of France in 1794–5, gave the Revolution his active support until as late as the summer of 1793, distributing trees from his estate to serve as totems of liberty, standing as godfather to the children of local patriots, playing a leading role in the local National Guard and standing for election to the National Convention.

By the time the Comte de Puisaye abandoned the Revolution, France had been plunged into the Terror of year II (1793–4). It was an episode which continues to generate intense controversy and a huge literature. It has been seen by Marxists such as Albert Soboul as the natural and inevitable climax of the Revolution, a time when the masses – led by the *sans-culottes* – drove the timid bourgeois on to complete the destruction of the feudal order [24]. For the post-revisionists, however, the Terror was not generated by social pressure but was the inevitable outcome of the Revolution's political culture. No part of their critique has been more controversial than this claim. It marked an abrupt change of heart on the part of François Furet. In his general history of the French Revolution, which he wrote in collaboration with Denis Richet and published in French in 1965 and in English translation in 1970, he presented the Terror as essentially an aberration, an exceptional reaction to an exceptional emergency. The military defeats of the spring of 1793, the consequent threat of foreign invasion, the sharply deteriorating economic situation and the counter-revolutionary insurrections all conspired to unleash a campaign of state terror to mobilise every last national resource, both human and material, in defence of the Revolution. Once that objective had been achieved, by the summer of 1794, the way was clear for a return to normality. As Furet and Richet wrote: 'Far from being an inevitable part of the revolutionary process, the dictatorship of Year II bears all the marks of contingency, of a nation that had found itself in dire straits' [6].

Compare that with Furet's verdict in his *Revolutionary France* published in 1988; 'the political culture which could lead to the Terror was present in the French Revolution right from the summer of 1789' [7]. The Terror developed inexorably, he argues, as part of a dialectic between the Revolution's primal demand for unity and its equally insistent belief in the existence of an aristocratic conspiracy. Its political culture was fundamentally non-pluralist, that is to say it could not contemplate the existence of honest disagreement: if there were divisions among the revolutionaries (as there patently always were), then this could only be the result of lies spread by counter-revolutionaries. Only by extirpating the enemy within could natural unanimity be restored. A similar if more direct interpretation of the Terror was offered by Simon Schama, who stressed that violence was at the heart of the Revolution right from the start: 'it was what made the Revolution revolutionary'. So the mass slaughter of year II was no aberration, rather it 'was merely 1789 with a higher body count' [10].

There is clearly much to be said for this post-revisionist analysis of the Terror. To assume that the Terror was just a knee-jerk reaction to a critical situation (and so can be excused on the grounds that desperate times require desperate measures) overlooks the awkward chronological fact that the Terror reached its height long after the military situation had been restored. The lack of pluralism in the political culture of the French Revolution did indeed clearly distinguish it from the British or American experience. The readiness of revolutionary politicians to condone or even encourage atrocities, if they appeared to further their aims, did give violence the status of normality. On the other hand, there was clearly a difference between the politics of 1789 and those of 1793–4. A recent examination of the judicial procedures of 1789–90 has found that the revolutionary authorities treated their opponents of both left and right with restraint and even leniency.

If there were indeed signs that pluralism was under strain, it did exist and there was a liberal phase of the Revolution [167]. It is also difficult to read – for example – Schama's brilliantly evocative if harrowing account of the Terror without feeling that this was a qualitatively as well as quantitatively different experience from that of 1789.

Part of the problem can be resolved if it is appreciated that the 'French Revolutionary Wars' did not begin in 1792 but in 1787. It was in August 1787 that a great systemic upheaval in the European states-system began, with the declaration of war on Russia by Turkey [11]. The French Revolution began as part of that upheaval and was decisively influenced by it from the start [Blanning in 9, 143]. For example, the 'Great Fear' or wave of violence which swept through the French countryside in the last two weeks of July 1789 and led to the abolition of the 'feudal regime' by the National Assembly was fuelled by the conviction that the war was about to come to France – that the Austrians would be invading from the north, the Swedes led by the Comte d'Artois from the north-east, the *émigrés* supported by German princes from the east, the Savoyards from the south-east, the Spanish from the south-west and the British from the sea [10]. This particular panic proved groundless, but conspiracy theories continued to grip the revolutionary imagination, not least because there *were* conspiracies afoot. In particular, the unashamedly counter-revolutionary activities of the *émigrés* ensured that the baleful interaction between domestic and international conflict would continue. As a result, revolutionary political culture was studded with references to the foreign situation, as for example in one of the most popular songs, 'Ça ira':

The Austrian slave will also die out,
Ah ça ira
And all their infernal gangs
Will fly off to the devil,
Ah ça ira.

Whether we regard the Terror as a temporary aberration or as an integral part of the Revolution's political culture, it is clear that its chief victims were bourgeois merchants and manufacturers. Indeed, further doubts about the bourgeois nature of the

Revolution are aroused when the beneficiaries are examined. They are difficult to find. Taking 1799 as one's vantage point, the only groups that can be said to have benefited in a material sense from the Revolution were purchasers of *biens nationaux* and the army (or, rather, those members of it who had won promotion and had survived). Certainly the bourgeois were to the fore in the former group. The original regulations were designed to favour small proprietors – purchasers had to find only 12 per cent of the price immediately and could pay off the rest in twelve annual instalments at 5 per cent interest. Subsequent changes increased the deposit, reduced the repayment period and increased the interest rate, with the result that only the richer peasants and, above all, the bourgeois were in a position to take advantage of the system [62]. As Denis Woronoff has pointed out, when the dust settled at the end of the 1790s: 'it was the merchants, industrialists, solicitors and lawyers who emerged victorious from this contest, with the not-disinterested help of the administrators of the *départements*' [169]. Yet, paradoxically, this bonanza only confirmed the French bourgeoisie's conservative predilection for proprietary wealth. The combination of the abolition of venal office and the availability of vast tracts of land only served to make land – rather than manufacturing, finance or commerce – even more popular for bourgeois investors.

Indeed, the economic conditions created by the Revolution were singularly unconducive to capitalist investment. Prominent on the long list of those who lost as a result of the Revolution were bourgeois capitalists, for whom the 1790s were years of great difficulty. A particular and enduring problem was the new regime's monetary policy. Galloping inflation, caused by the reckless printing of money, reached a climax in 1796 when it was costing more to print the *assignats* than they were worth. But the abandoning of paper money was followed by sharp deflation, a collapse of agricultural prices, a shortage of cash and high interest rates, causing problems for the business community which were different but just as intense [51].

The need to resort to paper money had been magnified greatly by the war, and it was the war which was mainly responsible for plunging the manufacturing sector into recession, by disrupting the supply of raw materials and by blocking access to foreign markets. From one textile manufacturing centre after another came the cry that output had fallen precipitously: Lyon had had 12,000 looms in 1789, but only 6,500 in 1802; Carcassonne's production had fallen from 60,000 rolls of cloth to just 17,000 or 18,000; by 1801 Le Mans had only 100 *métiers battants* left, compared with 274 in 1788, and production had declined in proportion; in the linen-producing regions of Brittany, production had fallen by at least a third in the course of the decade; the value of industrial production at Marseille fell by three-quarters after 1789, and so on [174]. The most recent historian of French textiles sums up as follows:

> The Revolution brought disaster to the French textile trade in every imaginable form: currency disorder, radical changes of fashion in clothing, loss of foreign customers, severe raw material shortages. Hundreds of thousands of cottagers were forced to abandon the trade; bankruptcy swallowed up hundreds of merchant houses [70].

That catalogue of disasters could be matched, and even added to, by merchants engaged in overseas trade. Once Great Britain had entered the war in February 1793, French ports were blockaded by the Royal Navy. The statistics illustrating the consequences are even more devastating than those relating to manufacturing: by 1797 there were only 200 ocean-going vessels left, a tenth of the 1789 total; by 1799 French exports amounted to 272 million francs, just half of the 1789 figure, even though in the meantime Belgium and its relatively advanced economy had been annexed; in 1789 foreign trade accounted for 25 per cent of the country's gross physical product, by 1796 it had fallen to 9 per cent; and so on [18, 163].

This sharp decline of manufacturing and commerce led to two phenomena known inelegantly as deindustrialisation and deurbanisation. Particularly in the industrial hinterland of those ports which had boomed during the eighteenth century there was a pronounced shift in the economic balance away from manufacturing [146]. The difficulty in finding alternative means of livelihood, especially at a time when the Revolution had eliminated so many forms of proprietary wealth, was reflected in the declining populations of major cities. Between 1789 and 1806 the population of Paris fell from more than 650,000 to 581,000, of Marseille from 110,000 to 99,000 and of Bordeaux from 110,000 to 93,000 [58].

It seems an odd sort of bourgeois revolution that can inflict such damage on the most advanced sector, economically speaking, of the bourgeoisie. This is an argument, however, which must be treated with caution. The revolutionaries who destroyed the old regime and erected the new did not know that in April 1792 they would become involved in a war which would last for the best part of a quarter of a century. On the contrary, the early pronouncements by the revolutionaries on the subject of foreign policy were entirely pacific. It was not until the autumn of 1791 that the possibility of war arose, thanks to the ambition of the Brissotins, the treachery of the Court and the miscalculations of the Austrians and the Prussians [142]. Once they found themselves 'trying to run a twentieth-century war effort with means available to a pre-industrial society' [150], as Norman Hampson has put it, the overexertion involved inevitably wreaked havoc with the economy. In short, one should not infer motives from consequences.

For post-revisionist historians such as François Furet or Lynn Hunt, to ask whether or not the Revolution promoted a bourgeois society and economy is *'une question mal posée'*. Now it is time to return to a remark made earlier, namely that the 'discursive forms' investigated by historians of political culture should not be regarded as mere reflections of underlying interests, but should be seen as real in themselves [see above p. 26]. Reacting against the Marxist dichotomy of socio-economic substructure and political (or cultural) superstructure, Furet and his followers have proclaimed the autonomy of politics. Their approach is not to follow the development of social classes or economic trends but to chart 'the importance of symbols, language, and ritual in inventing and transmitting a tradition of revolutionary action' [155]. The new political culture created so quickly in the crucible of the incinerating old regime was not driven by class conflict or even by a conflict between interest groups. Its extraordinary dynamism derived from a competition to appropriate the symbols of revolutionary legitimacy. On the one hand the revolutionaries believed with Rousseau that the power of the people could not be compromised by indirect representation through deputies. On the other hand, they had to recognise that in a country the size of France, direct democracy was impossible. The only way out of this dilemma was for the political leadership to present itself in such a way that its rhetoric embodied the popular will. That is why so much attention should be paid to the language, symbols and rituals – in a word, 'discourse' – of the Revolution, for that is where the secret of its development is to be found. In other words, the language and ritual of political struggle were not just the external symptoms of some deeper social reality, *they themselves were real*:

The Revolution . . . ushered in a world where mental representations of power governed all actions, and where a network of signs completely dominated political life. Politics was a matter of establishing just *who* represented the people, or equality, or the nation: victory was in the hands of those who were capable of occupying and keeping that symbolic position. The history of the Revolution between 1789 and 1794, in its period of development, can therefore be seen as the rapid drift from a compromise with the principle of representation toward the unconditional triumph of rule by opinion. It was a logical evolution, considering that the Revolution had from the outset made power out of opinion [35].

So revolutionary politics was a never-ending and mortal struggle over who was to interpret and express the people's will and it was this competition for discursive legitimacy which made the Revolution inherently unstable [132]. This has the appeal of inevitability but, once again, seems too determinist. In particular, it fails to take account of the destabilising force of the war. Most of the major upheavals of the 1790s – the rise of the Brissotins, the fall of the Brissotins, the fall of the monarchy, the *coup d'état* of Fructidor and the *coup d'état* of Brumaire – were caused in large measure by events at the front [143].

If politics can be given autonomy, so can gender. This is an approach to the Revolution which is still in its infancy, but has already yielded interesting if controversial results. One powerful line of argument holds that women were well on the way to emancipation during the closing years of the old regime, a process exemplified by their control of the salons. The decline of the latter in the 1780s and the emergence of exclusively male forms of sociability signalled a deterioration: 'The revolt against the monarchy in 1789 was prefigured by the revolt against salon governance in the 1780s, when the young male citizens of the Republic of Letters formed their own societies based on a fantasy of masculine self-governance which displaced women from their central governing role and restituted them as the objects of male desire and male learning' [108]. The Revolution then followed this masculine counter-attack through relegating women to second-class citizenship and suppressing any attempts they made to organise [156]. Napoleon then completed the process of subjugation with his notoriously sexist legal codes. There is much to be said for this gloomy scenario, although it is too neat to accommodate adequately the rich diversity of female experience in the 1790s. Women did find a way to intervene actively in revolutionary politics, never more so than during the October Days of 1789. They also benefited from the general expansion of the political space which the Revolution brought, often taking the lead in counter-revolutionary agitation, especially when it came to restoring traditional forms of religious worship [149].

3 Aftermath: Napoleon and Beyond

The development of France in the post-revolutionary period is characterised by what Georges Lefebvre described as a 'gigantic paradox'. Although the country had experienced 'the greatest revolution in the history of the world' (Karl Marx), in economic terms nothing seemed to have changed much. The political and social institutions of the old regime – the absolute monarchy, noble privileges, the established church – had been torn up by the roots, but the economy trundled along on its ponderous path more or less unaffected. It was all very well to blame the delay on the inevitable birth-pains of a new order or on the effects of the war, but such excuses were wearing thin a hundred years later, for – as Clive Trebilcock has written – 'by 1900 France was clearly the economic laggard among the powers and not even the unusually energetic progress of the *belle époque* could erase the languid and spasmodic growth pattern of the preceding century and a half' [186].

If the French bourgeoisie really had entered into their kingdom in 1789, then they took their time about exploiting their economic advantages, as the rates of growth achieved in France during the nineteenth century were substantially below those of other industrialising countries. Every attempt to argue that the French economy was not so backward after all [173] founders on the rock of relativity. In the course of the nineteenth century France fell behind the USA, Germany, Austria-Hungary and Russia in terms of population; in terms of total industrial production, France was overtaken by the USA, Germany and Great Britain and in terms of real income per capita by Switzerland, the Netherlands, Belgium, Scandinavia and several parts of the British Empire as well [68, 172]. Contemplation of the superior growth rates achieved by the economies of Great Britain and Germany, where so many features of the old regime survived, suggests that when it came to industrialisation, a revolution of the French variety was at best an irrelevance and at worst a handicap.

The temptation to view the Revolution as anti-capitalist in its consequences must be tempered by the consideration that the pace of industrialisation in France might have been even more lethargic without it. Great Britain and Germany, after all, enjoyed superior natural communications and superior natural resources. Nevertheless, it does seem clear that, from being roughly on a par economically on the eve of the Revolution, France and Great Britain had diverged appreciably by 1815. The economic recovery of the Napoleonic Empire had been just that – recovery to the old regime's levels of output after a decade of deprivation [184]. Many of the industries which flourished – notably textiles – could do so only in the artificial conditions created by protective tariffs and the economic domination of the rest of the continent that went with French military hegemony. When the rest of Europe regained its independence and when British goods regained access to French markets, the hothouse flowers (already nipped back by the sharp recessions of 1810–11 and 1813–14) withered accordingly. As François Crouzet has concluded: 'France was not disastrously behind [in the 1780s], and the Industrial Revolution might have taken off there with only a few years' delay in relation to England. But the "national catastrophe" which the French Revolution and the twenty years war meant to the French economy would intensify the discrepancy and make it irremediable' [54].

The negative effects of the 'national catastrophe' were enduring. The 1,300,000 Frenchmen lost as a result of the wars between 1792 and 1815 left the country with a low male/female ratio (down from 0.992 in 1790 to 0.857 in 1815) and a falling share of Europe's population [58]. The agrarian policies of the Revolution only served to confirm and consolidate the predominance of peasant proprietors aiming just at subsistence agriculture [45]. The bitter legacy of political and social polarisation, which brought repeated violent changes of regime and a persistent sense of instability, almost certainly helps to explain the fabled and fatal reluctance of Frenchmen to invest in domestic enterprise. The contrast in this regard with Great Britain (or even Germany) in the same period is both striking and instructive.

It is just this constant reference to the contrasting experience of the British economy which has attracted the criticism of a group of Marxist-Leninist historians. The most influential of them has been Anatoly Ado, whose *magnum opus* – a study of peasant movements in France between 1789 and 1794 published in 1971 [42] – has not been translated from its original Russian but has been immensely influential. It was Ado's invaluable service to his Marxist-Leninist colleagues to demonstrate how the 'gigantic paradox' which had troubled Georges Lefebvre could be overcome. Indeed, he was sharply critical of certain important aspects of Lefebvre's work on the peasants. In particular, he argued that Lefebvre had been quite wrong to conclude that the peasant revolution was not an integral part of the bourgeois revolution. In Ado's view, that fundamental error had led Lefebvre to the equally mistaken conclusion that the peasants' programme was in many respects hostile to economic progress and that therefore the peasant revolution had been – and this was the 'gigantic paradox', of course – both revolutionary and conservative [42].

Ado resolved the problem by distinguishing between the subjective and the objective roles of the peasantry. In a subjective sense, the peasants' deeds and words may have appeared to have been anti-capitalist, backward–looking, designed to protect their traditional communal rights and structures. But *objectively*, by demanding, fighting for and eventually achieving the total destruction of feudalism, the peasants opened the way for the triumph of capitalism. It was the democratic, egalitarian way, but it was the way to capitalism just the same. Their creation of free peasant property led to a differentiation between property-owners and labourers and the possibility of capital accumulation. Ado was also at pains to stress the crucial importance of the peasant movement. It was no separate epiphenomenon but the true motor of the Revolution, right from the very start: 'the popular movements played the most decisive, dynamic role in bringing about the development of the revolutionary crisis [in 1788–9] and its transformation into a revolution' [42].

So, far from being a conservative force, the peasant movements in France were as radical as it was possible to be. The English revolution of the seventeenth century had abolished only the feudal ties of the great magnates, leaving those of the peasants intact. Copyhold was not recognised as the peasants' property and so the basis was laid for their later expropriation and 'landlordism'. The French Revolution of 1789, on the other hand, decisively destroyed the entire feudal structure and unleashed violence, not against the peasantry (as in England) but against the feudal – i.e. seigneurial – aristocrats. And not only did it liberate the peasants from all feudal ties, but it also expanded their total holdings by the division of commons and the sale of the *biens nationaux* [43].

This ingenious theoretical exercise, which had the outstanding merit of both confirming the French Revolution as a bourgeois revolution at the same time as it elevated the role of the masses at the expense of the bourgeoisie itself, was eagerly taken up by Albert Soboul and his pupils. Soboul's own methodological odyssey, at each stage along the way according more importance to the peasants, has been chronicled by Christof Dipper: in his general history of the Revolution, published in 1962, Soboul just remarked that within the general framework of the Revolution there developed a peasant current; in 1969 he was still writing only of a 'bourgeois revolution' in which 'popular classes have been the motor'; but in 1971 he stated that 'peasants and the popular revolution in fact stood at the centre of the bourgeois revolution and drove it forwards'; in his review of Ado's book he went so far as to abandon the phrase 'bourgeois revolution' in favour of 'peasant-bourgeois revolution'; finally, in 1978, he went the whole hog and called it a 'peasant revolution' which had forced a bourgeois revolution in the countryside and thus opened the way for capitalism [55].

No great acumen is required to spot that Ado and his French supporters have 1917 just as much as 1789 in view. That is why Lenin rather than Marx has proved so much more helpful as a source of supportive theoretical quotations. Ado does his gallant best to enlist the support of the master and Soboul has exclaimed testily: 'For my part, I have never considered *Das Kapital* to be the Bible nor Marx to be a prophet. One will always find quotations of Marx, Engels, Lenin and – why not? – Stalin and Mao, to oppose to other quotations' [27]. Significantly, Soboul made that observation in the course of berating Marxist heresy.

But no matter how much ingenuity is exercised in selecting what to quote and what to explain away, the obstinate fact remains that Marx had a very low opinion of peasants. In his view, the peasant was doomed just because he was a peasant, his imminent demise an inevitable consequence of progress and not to be regretted, for the peasant was engaged in 'the most primitive and irrational form of exploitation'. An economy based on peasants was bound to make the people chained to it 'a class of barbarians', 'uniting in itself all the crudeness of primitive social forms with all the tortures and all the misery of modern society'. No amount of planing and smoothing can make observations by Marx such as the following fit the Ado-Soboul version of the French Revolution: 'The evil to which the French peasant is succumbing is just his dwarf-holding, the partition of the soil, the form of tenure which Napoleon consolidated in France' [20].

As Soboul observed, Marxist scripture should not be treated as if it were Holy Writ, least of all by an agnostic. However, there are more substantive objections to be raised against the notion of a peasant revolution that was really bourgeois. So much of the peasant activity after 1789 was explicitly *counter*-revolutionary in character that the gap between subjective perceptions and objective roles is stretched much too far to be credible. Significantly, Soboul and his followers have paid virtually no attention to the counter-revolution, which has been placed by revisionists at the very centre of the stage, a mass movement comparable in scope to the Revolution itself [12].

The Marxists have a fair point when they stress that what really matters about late-eighteenth-century 'feudalism' is the meaning attached to it by contemporary peasants and not its actual (and minimal) relationship to its medieval ancestor [22]. But they then inflate its scope and meaning well beyond anything those peasants would have recognised. As one regional study after another has demonstrated, the insurgents were not just revolting against feudalism (or rather the seigneurial system) and even where they did so, it was not so much the seigneurial dues themselves to which they took exception as their commercial exploitation. They rose not against a reactionary feudal aristocracy but in defence of a pre-capitalist economic system based on small peasant holdings and against the tendency towards agrarian capitalism displayed by their seigneurs, an increasing number of whom were urban bourgeois [62, 67]. In short, the peasant revolution was not for capitalism but against it.

Against the seductive argument that this last conclusion is valid only on a subjective level and that 'objectively' – in spite of themselves – the peasants were on the side of progress, it is necessary only to consider the actual development of French agriculture in the following century. What Ado and his followers fail to take into account is the inescapable fact that the peasants freed from the fetters of feudalism wanted nothing more than self-subsistence and sought to avoid the risks involved in commercial farming. Moreover, and *objectively*, the opportunities for most of them were strictly limited by the old obstacle of poor communications. It was not until the transport revolution, which began in the middle of the nineteenth century with the construction of the railways, that the opportunity to specialise and the incentive to produce a marketable surplus were created. Agricultural production was probably lower in 1820 than it had been in the 1780s.

As Maurice Garden has observed, until the Second Empire the agrarian history of France in the nineteenth century was largely a repetition of the eighteenth century: only the railways and the concentration of population in towns brought change. They, not the Revolution of 1789, were the real destroyers of the old regime in the country [60]. The legislation of the Revolution had changed the legal status of the peasants – and may even have improved the material status of the minority lucky enough to own their own land – but on the way of life and way of thinking of the great mass of the rural population, it had had no effect.

If the Revolution neither established nor accelerated but probably delayed the development of capitalism in France [31], a closer look at the social dimension also raises doubts about its radicalism. On the face of it, the abolition of the nobility, the abolition of the seigneurial regime, the abolition of venality, the expropriation of the *émigrés*, the introduction of egalitarian legal codes and the establishment of a meritocracy should have led to a change of elites. In the event, once the turmoil of the mid-1790s had died down, it turned out that there had been little change. When, in 1802, Napoleon's prefects compiled the electoral lists which in effect were surveys of local notables, they established that most of the wealthiest landowners in France were still the nobles of the old regime [170]. Recanting an earlier view, Robert Forster has commented: 'large landlords of the Old Regime, noble or not, were not destroyed – nor even permanently hurt – by the Revolution' [177]. Napoleon may have talked about a field-marshal's baton in every private's knapsack, but in practice he preferred to rely on men of independent and well-established means. The only major change he made to the traditional structure was to increase the number and improve the status of civil servants. The result was that the mixed elite of nobles and commoners which had been in the process of formation during the eighteenth century was now firmly established. As Robert Forster has concluded:

> The elite that governed France after the Revolution and owed so much to the conscious policies of Napoleon was essentially a notability of landlords and *hauts fonctionnaires*, with smaller con tingents of lawyers, merchants, and manufacturers – smaller in both number and influence. This elite was drawn from the old noble families as well as from newcomers, a successful amalgam of wealth, education, family connections, local influence, and political power. Without legal privileges and placing less weight on birth, it saw itself as a service elite, the rule of the *capacités*. Drawn from many of the same families who had administered France in the Old Regime, the new notables evolved a common set of social values and attitudes that were appropriate to their own time and place. They governed France, with a few brief interruptions, from 1800–1880 and even beyond [177].

One is tempted to append the comment *Plus ça change, plus c'est la même chose*, but this would be too immobile a note on which to end. As it was essentially political, the French Revolution certainly had a tremendous impact on the politics not only of France but of the world. Soboul and his Marxist-Leninist colleagues felt obliged to give pre-eminence to the Russian Revolution of 1917, but after the events of 1989, this status will prove difficult to sustain. Two centuries of tried and tested political impact surely puts the French Revolution in pole position. This has been argued cogently by one of the most impressive and influential of the post-revisionist works, Lynn Hunt's *Politics, Culture and Class in the French Revolution*:

> The chief accomplishment of the French Revolution was the institution of a dramatically new political culture . . . Revolution in France contributed little to economic growth or to political stabilisation. What it did establish was the mobilising potential of democratic republicanism and the compelling intensity of revolutionary change . . . Industrial capitalism still grew at a

snail's pace. In the realm of politics, in contrast, almost everything changed. Thousands of men and even many women gained firsthand experience in the political arena: they talked, read, and listened in new ways; they voted; they joined new organisations; and they marched for their political goals. Revolution became a tradition, and republicanism an enduring option. Afterward, kings could not rule without assemblies, and noble domination of public affairs only provoked more revolution. As a result, France in the nineteenth century had the most bourgeois polity in Europe, even though France was never the leading industrial power [154].

One reason why France never became the leading industrial power was the chronic instability which was part and parcel of the Revolution's democratic political culture. There were abrupt changes of regime in 1799, 1814, 1815 (twice), 1830, 1848, 1851 and 1870. Even the Third Republic had to overcome several existential crises. It is only very recently, if at all, that the actual regime has ceased to be a political issue. It is doubtful whether the Fifth Republic will be the last, if only because 200 years of history suggest otherwise. This restlessness highlights the contrast between the non-pluralist unanimity which the Revolution demanded and the intense polarisation which it actually created. The only escape has proved to be rule by an authoritarian, charismatic leader, supported by democratic rhetoric and ritual. So the main achievement of the Revolution was not to make the world safe for the bourgeoisie but for Bonapartism. In the concluding words of what is both the most recent and the most penetrating analysis of post-revolutionary France:

De Gaulle's Fifth Republic, the first political system since the Revolution to have attained practically universal acceptance, is a new version, shorn of dynastic complications, of the Bonapartist formula of the 'republican monarch', 'the only chance for French democracy' (Michel Debré). In short, it is not the revolution in its 'weak', liberal parliamentary form – 'the principles of 1789' – that has concluded the long post-revolutionary ordeal, but that characteristic French combination of 'active authority and passive democracy' first exploited by Bonaparte [185].

Select Bibliography

There is space to list only those works actually cited in the text, together with a handful of others found particularly useful. The best way for a student to keep up to date with French Revolutionary historiography is through the works listed in the periodical *French Historical Studies*. Exhaustive is the *Bibliographie annuelle de l'histoire de France* (Paris, 1953–).

Historiography

[1]   W. Doyle, *Origins of the French Revolution*, 2nd edn (1988). This admirably concise and lucid study supersedes all previous historiographical surveys. A third edition is now needed.
[2]   R. Reichardt, 'Bevölkerung und Gesellschaft Frankreichs im 18. Jahrhundert: neue Wege und Ergebnisse der sozialhistorischen Forschung 1950–1976', *Zeitschrift für historische Forschung*, IV (1977). A long, full and very valuable bibliographical survey.
[3]   M. Vovelle (ed.), *L'Image de la Révolution française. Communications présentées lors du Congrès Mondial pour le Bicentenaire de la Révolution Sorbonne Paris 6–12 juillet 1989*, 4 vols (1990). Proceedings of the conference on the French Revolution to end them all, containing nearly 300 papers.

General Works

[4]   T. C. W. Blanning (ed.), *The rise and fall of the French Revolution* (1996). Seventeen trail-blazing articles which first appeared in the *Journal of Modern History*, plus historiographical introduction.
[5]   W. Doyle, *The Oxford History of the French Revolution* (1989). An excellent blend of narrative and analysis, well-balanced, judicious but also a very good read.
[6]   F. Furet and D. Richet, *The French Revolution* (1977). Well-illustrated, revisionist account.

[7]   F. Furet, *Revolutionary France* 1770–1880 (1992). Occasionally
        pretentious but usually intelligent and penetrating.
[8]   Peter Jones (ed.), *The French Revolution in Social and Political
        Perspective* (1996). A very useful anthology of extracts from vari-
        ous historians, marred by total neglect of the international
        dimension.
[9]   C. Lucas (ed.), *Rewriting the French Revolution* (1991). Eight lec-
        tures given in Oxford in 1989.
[10]   S. Schama, *Citizens. A chronicle of the French Revolution* (1989).
        Brilliant and compulsively readable; controversially argues that
        at the heart of the Revolution was violence.
[11]   Paul W. Schroeder, *The Transformation of European Politics
        1763–1848* (1994). Massive but wonderfully readable, this puts
        the primacy of foreign policy back where it belongs and is essen-
        tial reading for anyone wishing to understand the French
        Revolution.
[12]   D. Sutherland, *France 1789–1815* (1985). Particularly good on
        the counter-revolution, which is placed on an equal footing with
        the Revolution itself.

Marxist and Marxist-Leninist Interpretations

[13]   G. Comninel, *Rethinking the French Revolution: Marxism and the
        revisionist challenge* (1987). A difficult read but shows that there
        is life in the old interpretation yet.
[14]   F. Furet, *Marx and the French Revolution* (1988). A study of Marx's
        writings on the French Revolution, accompanied by appropriate
        texts by Marx.
[15]   M. Grenon and R. Robin, 'A propos de la polémique sur l'ancien
        régime et la Révolution: pour une problématique de la transi-
        tion', *La Pensée*, CLXXXVII (1976). Lively polemical attack on
        revisionists such as Chaussinand-Nogaret and Furet, but also crit-
        ical of Soboul.
[16]   C. Jones, 'Bourgeois revolution revivified: 1789 and social
        change', in [9]. Ingenious but not wholly convincing attempt to
        revive the 'bourgeois' interpretation by a non-Marxist.
[17]   G. Lefebvre, *The Coming of the French Revolution* (1947). Still one
        of the best introductions to the subject.
[18]   G. Lefebvre, *The French Revolution from its Origins to 1793* (1962)
        and *The French Revolution from 1793 to 1799* (1964). First pub-
        lished more than fifty years ago, this general history remains
        stimulating and informative. Surprisingly good on foreign policy.
[19]   G. Lefebvre, 'The place of the Revolution in the agrarian histo-
        ry of France', in R. Forster and O. Ranum (eds), *Rural Society in
        France* (1977). Unlike Soboul, he sees the peasants in 1789 as
        essentially conservative.

[20]   D. Mitrany, *Marx Against the Peasant – a Study in Social Dogmatism*
        (1951). Shows how much Marx despised the peasantry.
[21]   E. Schmitt and M. Meyn, *Ursprung und Charakter der
        Französischen Revolution bei Marx und Engels* (1976). A very help-
        ful account and analysis of the views of Marx and Engels on the
        French Revolution.
[22]   A. Soboul, *La Civilisation et la Révolution française* (1970). The
        definitive statement of Soboul's views on the Enlightenment and
        the Revolution.
[23]   A. Soboul, 'Classes and class struggles during the French
        Revolution', *Science and Society*, 17 (1953). A convenient summa-
        ry of Soboul's early views.
[24]   A. Soboul, *The French Revolution 1787–1799. From the storming of
        the Bastille to Napoleon* (1974). The most accessible work by
        Soboul in English but superseded by his later work.
[25]   A. Soboul, 'L'historiographie classique de la Révolution
        française', *Historical Reflections – Réflexions historiques*, I (1974).
        Perhaps the most thoughtful of Soboul's replies to the revisionists.
[26]   A. Soboul, 'Problèmes théoriques de l'histoire de la Révolution
        française', *La Nouvelle Critique*, XLIII (1971).
[27]   A. Soboul, 'Sur l'article de Michel Grenon et Régine Robin', *La
        Pensée*, CLXXXVII (1976). Critical of a Marxist but 'gradualist'
        view of revolution.
[28]   A. Soboul. 'Sur le mouvement paysan dans la Révolution
        française', *La Pensée*, CLXVIII (1973). Summarises and com-
        mends the views of Anatoly Ado.
[29]   V. P. Volguine, 'L'idéologie révolutionnaire en France au XVIIIe
        siècle: ses contradictions et son évolution', *La Pensée*, LXXXVI
        (1959). Trenchantly expressed views of a Soviet historian.

Revisionist Criticism

[30]   G. Chaussinand-Nogaret, 'Aux origines de la Révolution:
        noblesse et bourgeoisie', *Annales. Économies, Sociétés, Civilisations*,
        XXX (1975). One of the most spirited attacks on Marxist ortho-
        doxy.
[31]   A. Cobban, *The Social Interpretation of the French Revolution*
        (1964). The Wiles lectures of 1962, which became the most
        important single manifesto of the revisionists.
[32]   E. Eisenstein, 'Who intervened in 1788?', *American Historical
        Review*, LXXI (1965). Has one important point to make.
[33]   W. Doyle, 'Was there an aristocratic reaction in pre-revolutionary
        France?', *Past and Present*, LVII (1972). A very important piece;
        argues convincingly that there was none.
[34]   G. Ellis, 'The "Marxist interpretation" of the French Revolution',
        English Historical Review, XCIII (1978). A penetrating and effec-
        tive critique.

[35]   F. Furet, *Interpreting the French Revolution* (1981). This collection
         includes his celebrated attack on Soboul and also marks the
         beginning of the post-revisionist phase.
[36]   C. Lucas, 'Nobles, bourgeois and the origins of the French
         Revolution', *Past and Present*, LX (1973). This has proved to be
         one of the most influential of the revisionist attacks.
[37]   E. Schmitt, 'Einleitung' to his anthology *Die Französische
         Revolution* (1977).
[38]   G. V. Taylor, 'The bourgeoisie at the beginning of and during the
         French Revolution', in Eberhard Schmitt and Rolf Reichardt
         (eds), *Die Französische Revolution – zufälliges oder notwendiges
         Ereignis?* (1983). Argues that the Revolution was due to the coin-
         cidence of a political crisis with a socio-economic crisis.
[39]   G. V. Taylor, 'Noncapitalist wealth and the origins of the French
         Revolution', *American Historical Review*, LXXXII (1967). A very
         important article which argues that there was more in old-regime
         France to unite the nobility and bourgeoisie than to divide them.
[40]   G. V. Taylor, 'Types of capitalism in eighteenth-century France',
         English Historical Review, LXXIX (1964).
[41]   G. V. Taylor, 'Bourgeoisie', in Samuel F. Scott and Barry Rothaus
         (eds), *Historical Dictionary of the French Revolution 1789–1799*,
         vol. I (1984). Helpful discussion of possible definitions.

         See also [145 (b), (c), (d)].

The Ancien Régime

(See also the bibliography in William Doyle's *The Ancien Régime*
published in this series.)

Economy and society

[42]   A. Ado, *Krest'yanskoe dvizhenie vo Frantsii vo vremya velikoy burzhi-
         aznoy revoliutsii kontsa XVIII veka* (1971). An imaginative Marxist-
         Leninist work on the peasant revolution which has exerted a
         strong influence on Albert Soboul and his pupils.
[43]   A. Ado, 'Krest'yanskie vosstaniya i likvidatsiya feodal'nykh povi-
         nostey vo vremya frantsuzkhoy burzhuanznoy revoliutsii kontsa
         XVIII v.', in M. Kossok (ed.), *Studien über die Revolution*, 2nd edn
         (1971). A short article, but easier to obtain than his main work,
         which is something of a bibliographical rarity.
[44]   A. Ado, 'Le mouvement paysan et le problème de l'égalité
         (1789–1794)', in A. Soboul (ed.), *Contributions à l'histoire*

paysanne de la Révolution française (1977). Unfortunately for those who do not read Russian, not a translation of [42].

[45]   F. Aftalion, *The French Revolution: an economic interpretation* (1990). Excellent on the fiscal problems of both old regime and Revolution.

[46]   C. B. A. Behrens, 'Government and society', in E. Rich and C. Wilson (eds), *The Cambridge Economic History of Europe*, vol. V (1997). A penetrating and wide-ranging essay which places France in its European context.

[47]   C. B. A. Behrens, 'Nobles, privileges and taxes at the end of the Ancien Régime', *Economic History Review*, XV (1962–3). Argues that despite formal exemptions, the French nobles *were* taxed.

[48]   L. Bergeron, 'L'économie française sous le feu de la Révolution politique et sociale', in P. Léon (ed.), *Histoire économique et sociale du monde*, vol. III: *Inerties et révolutions (1730–1840)* (1978).

[49]   David Bien, 'La réaction aristocratique: l'exemple de l'armée', *Annales. Économies, Sociétés, Civilisations*, XXIX, 1 (1974). Much wider-ranging than the title suggests, shows how easy it was to become a noble in old-regime France.

[50]   M. Bloch, 'La lutte pour l'individualisme agraire dans la France du XVIIIe siècle', *Annales. Économies, Sociétés, Civilisations*, II (1930). Still very important for understanding why French agriculture changed so little during the eighteenth century.

[51]   F. Braudel and E. Labrousse (eds), *Histoire économique et sociale de la France*, vol. II: *Des derniers temps de l'âge seigneurial aux préludes de l'âge industriel (1660–1789)* (1970).

[52]   G. Chaussinand-Nogaret, *The French Nobility in the Eighteenth Century* (1985). A brilliant blend of insights and polemics.

[53]   N. F. R. Crafts, 'Macroinventions, economic growth and "industrial revolution" in Britain and France', *Economic History Review*, XLVIII, 3 (1995). Argues that actual British growth rates in the eighteenth century were not appreciably higher but concedes that French growth potential was lower.

[54]   F. Crouzet, 'England and France in the eighteenth century: a comparative analysis of two economic growths', in R. M. Hartwell (ed.), *The Causes of the Industrial Revolution in England* (1967). Shows that France was not so far behind England in 1789 in terms of industrialisation as has been often supposed.

[55]   C. Dipper, 'Die Bauern in der französischen Revolution', *Geschichte und Gesellschaft*, VII (1981). A very useful bibliographical essay.

[56]   W. Doyle, *The Ancien Régime* (1986). Lucid and cogent essay, particularly strong on the historiography of the old regime.

[57]   W. Doyle, *The Old European Order* (1978). Excellent general study which puts France in a European perspective.

[58]   J. Dupâquier, *La population française au XVIIe et XVIIIe siècle* (1979). The most authoritative review of the fragmentary evidence relating to French population in the period.

[59]   R. Forster, 'The middle classes in eighteenth-century western
         Europe', in J. Schneider (ed.), *Wirtschaftskräfte und
         Wirtschaftswege: Festschrift für Hermann Kellenbenz*, vol. III (1978).
         A very helpful discussion of what 'bourgeois' meant to contem-
         poraries.
[60]   M. Garden, 'Un procès: la "révolution agricole" en France', in P.
         Léon (ed.), *Histoire économique et sociale du monde*, vol. III: *Inerties
         et révolutions (1730–1840)* (1978). Shows how limited was agri-
         cultural change in eighteenth-century France.
[61]   P. Goubert, *The Ancien Régime*, 2 vols (1962, 1973). English trans-
         lation of vol. I available. Particularly good on the social and eco-
         nomic aspects of the old regime.
[62]   G. van den Heuvel, *Grundprobleme der französischen Bauernschaft
         1730–1794* (1982). A short but penetrating and very helpful sur-
         vey.
[63]   E. Hinrichs, E Schmitt and R. Vierhaus (eds), *Vom Ancien Régime
         zur französischen Revolution. Forschungen und Perspektive* (1978).
         An exceptionally valuable collection of conference papers.
[64]   O. Hufton, *The Poor of Eighteenth-century France* (1974). A mas-
         terpiece of social history.
[65]   O. Hufton, 'The seigneur and the rural community in eigh-
         teenth-century France. The seigneurial reaction: a reappraisal',
         Transactions of the Royal Historical Society, 5th series, XXIX (1979).
         Demonstrates that the seigneurial system had its positive side.
[66]   V. Hunecke, 'Antikapitalistische Strömungen in der französischen
         Revolution', *Geschichte und Gesellschaft*, IV (1978). Thoughtful, but
         not an easy read; particularly good on the peasants.
[67]   E. Le Roy Ladurie, 'Révoltes et contestations rurales en France
         de 1675 à 1788', *Annales. Économies, Sociétés, Civilisations*, XXIX
         (1974). An exceedingly valuable review article, which discusses
         monographs by Saint-Jacob, Poitrineau, Meyer and others.
[68]   D. Landes, 'What room for accident?: explaining big changes by
         small events', *Economic History Review*, XLVII (1996). Analyses
         French backwardness.
[69]   P. Mathias, 'Concepts of Revolution in England and France in
         the eighteenth century', *Studies in Eighteenth-Century Culture*,
         XIV (1975). A very illuminating comparison of the fiscal systems
         of the two countries.
[70]   W. M. Reddy, *The Rise of Market Culture. The Textile Trade and
         French Society 1750–1900* (1984). A major study, much wider in
         range than the title suggests.
[71]   M. Sonenscher, *Work and Wages: Natural Law, Politics and the
         Eighteenth-century French Trades* (1989). From a highly original
         perspective sheds all sorts of new light on old-regime society.
[72]   D. R. Weir, 'Les crises économiques et les origines de la
         Révolution française', *Annales. Économies, Sociétés, Civilisations*,
         XLVI, 4 (1991). Argues that the negative effects of demographic
         growth before 1789 have been exaggerated and that the crisis of
         1788–9 was not inevitable.

Government and politics

[73]   M. Antoine, *Louis XV* (Paris, 1989). A mine of information and a
        good read, but too generous to its subject and unduly critical of
        the *parlements*.
[74]   C. B. A. Behrens, *Society, Government and the Enlightenment: the
        experiences of eighteenth-century France and Prussia* (1985). A
        revealing comparison of two very different states.
[75]   T. C. W. Blanning, 'Louis XV and the decline of the French
        monarchy', *History Review*, 22 (1995). Argues that a combination
        of foreign failure and the 'sleaze factor' delegitimated the
        monarchy.
[76]   J. F. Bosher, *French Finances 1775–1795. From Business to
        Bureaucracy* (1970). Argues that the monarchy's financial prob-
        lems did not stem from fiscal exemptions.
[77]   J. S. Bromley, 'The decline of absolute monarchy', in J. Wallace-
        Hadrill and J. McManners (eds), *France: Government and Society*,
        2nd edn (1970). A stimulating essay which stresses the destabil-
        ising role of the *parlements*
[78]   J. Collins, *The State in Early Modern France* (1995). The best
        introduction.
[79]   J. Delmas (ed.), *De 1715 à 1871*, in André Corvisier (ed.),
        Histoire militaire de la France, vol. II: (1992). The contributors to
        this volume show how important military affairs in their widest
        sense were and that historians neglect them at their peril. Also
        relevant for the revolutionary period.
[80]   W. Doyle, *Venality. The Sale of Offices in Eighteenth-century France*
        (1996). A very important and original study which shows how
        central venality was in pre-revolutionary France.
[81]   W. Doyle, 'The parlements of France and the breakdown of the
        old régime, 1771–1788', *French Historical Studies*, 13 (1970).
        Argues persuasively that Maupeou's reforms were essentially a
        political manoeuvre to get rid of Choiseul.
[82]   W. Doyle, 'The Parlements', in K. M. Baker (ed.), *The French
        Revolution and the Creation of Modern Political Culture*, vol. II: *The
        Political Culture of the French Revolution*, ed. C. Lucas (1988).
[83]   D. Echeverria, *The Maupeou Revolution: a Study in the History of
        Libertarianism, France, 1770–1774* (1985).
[84]   J. Hardman, *Louis XVI* (1993). Excellent biography; especially
        good on court politics.
[85]   Sarah Maza, 'The diamond necklace affair revisited
        (1785–1786): the case of the missing queen', in Lynn Hunt
        (ed.), *Eroticism and the body politic* (1991). The great scandal of
        the closing years of the old regime, thought by no less a person
        than Goethe to be the cause of the Revolution.
[86]   M. Price, *Preserving the Monarchy: the comte de Vergennes,
        1774–1787* (1995). Excellent and well-written account of court
        intrigue and the contribution it made to the destabilisation of
        the monarchy.

[87]   J. Swann, *Politics and the Parlement of Paris under Louis XV,
       1754–1774* (1996). Lucid, cogent and well researched, the best
       book in any language on the parlementary opposition to Louis
       XV.
[88]   D. K. Van Kley, *The Damiens affair and the Unravelling of the Ancien
       Régime* (1984).
[89]   D. Van Kley, 'The church, state and the ideological origins of the
       French Revolution', *Journal of Modern History*, 51/4 (1979),
       reprinted in [4]. Stresses the role played by Jansenism and the
       parlements.
[90]   J. de Viguerie, 'Le roi et le "public". L'exemple de Louis XV',
       Revue historique, 563 (1987). A very revealing article which shows
       how Louis XV lost control of the court.
[91]   E. Weber, 'Das Sacre Ludwigs XVI. vom 11. Juni 1775 und die
       Krise des Ancien Régime', in E. Hinrichs, E. Schmitt and R.
       Vierhaus (eds), *Vom Ancien Régime zur französischen Revolution.
       Forschungen und Ergebnisse* (1978). Shows how outdated was
       Louis XVI's notion of kingship.

The Enlightenment

[92]   L. Althusser, *Montesquieu, Rousseau, Marx. Politics and history*
       (1982). Unorthodox and stimulating Marxist analysis.
[93]   K. M. Baker, 'French political thought at the accession of Louis
       XVI', *Journal of Modern History*, 50/2 (1978), pp. 279–303. and
       reprinted in [4]. Complements [91] in an interesting way.
[94]   K. M. Baker, 'On the problem of the ideological origins of the
       French Revolution', in K. M. Baker, *Inventing the French
       Revolution* (1990).
[95]   J. R. Censer, *The French Press in the Age of Enlightenment* (1994).
       Very useful on the rise in circulation and the nature of reader-
       ship. Also shows that there was more royalist discourse than
       many have supposed.
[96]   R. Chartier, *The Cultural Origins of the French Revolution* (1991).
       Cogent and lucid essays.
[97]   R. Darnton, *The Business of Enlightenment. A Publishing History of
       the Encyclopédie 1775–1800* (1979). A very long technical
       account, but the last fifty pages are of general interest.
[98]   R. Darnton, 'In search of Enlightenment: recent attempts to cre-
       ate a social history of ideas', *Journal of Modern History*, 43 (1971).
[99]   R. Darnton, *The Great Cat Massacre and Other Episodes in French
       Cultural History* (1985). A bran-tub.
[100] R. Darnton, 'An enlightened revolution?', *The New York Review of
       Books*, 24 October 1991. A critical review of the work of Baker
       and Chartier.
[101] R. Darnton, *The Forbidden Best-sellers of Pre-Revolutionary France*
       (1996). A *plaidoyer* for the importance of pornography.

[102]   R. Darnton, 'The high enlightenment and the low life of litera-
         ture in pre-revolutionary France', *Past and Present*, 51 (1971).
         Influential and revealing examination of the radical gutter press
         of pre-revolutionary France.
[103]   R. Darnton, 'Reading, writing and publishing in eighteenth-cen-
         tury France: a case-study in the sociology of literature', *Daedalus*,
         100 (1971).
[104]   E. Eisenstein, *Grub Street Abroad: Aspects of the French Cosmopolitan
         Press from the Age of Louis XV to the French Revolution* (1992).
         Adopting a wide perspective, she shows that the alleged gulf
         between the 'high enlightenment' and '*Grub Street*' has been
         greatly exaggerated.
[105]   P. Gay, *The Enlightenment: an Interpretation*, vol. 1: *The Rise of
         Modern Paganism* (1967), vol. 2: *The Science of Freedom* (1969).
         Elegant, wordy, Whig account of the Enlightenment.
[106]   P. Gay, *Voltaire's Politics* (n.d.). The best of Gay's books, it relates
         the development of Voltaire's political thought to his response to
         specific incidents.
[107]   P. Gay, 'Why was the enlightenment?', in Peter Gay (ed.),
         Eighteenth-Century Studies (1975). Sharply critical of Marxist
         interpretations of the Enlightenment.
[108]   D. Goodman, 'Enlightenment salons: the convergence of female
         and philosophic ambitions', *Eighteenth-Century Studies*, 22, 3
         (1989). Perhaps exaggerates the importance of the salons but
         has a good point to make.
[109]   D. Goodman, *The Republic of Letters. A Cultural History of the
         French Enlightenment* (1994). Excellent on the social context,
         stressing especially the crucial role played by women. Sharply
         critical of Darnton.
[110]   N. Hampson, 'Grub Street revolutionaries', *The New York Review
         of Books*, 7 October 1982. Attack on Darnton.
[111]   N. Hampson, 'The Enlightenment in France', in R. Porter (ed.),
         The Enlightenment in National Context (1981). An essay full of
         sharp insights and telling comparisons between France and
         England.
[112]   R. Koselleck, *Critique and Crisis. Enlightenment and the Pathogenesis
         of Modern Society* (1987). As the title suggests, a very difficult read
         in any language, but possibly worth it.
[113]   J. Lough, *The Contributors to the Encyclopédie* (1973).
         Demonstrates that a wide cross-section of French society was
         involved.
[114]   J. Lough, *An Introduction to Eighteenth-century France* (1960).
         Unjustly neglected, one of the best books on culture and society
         in pre-revolutionary France.
[115]   J. Lough, *The Encyclopédie* (1971). Helpful guide to the most
         important single publication of the French Enlightenment.
[116]   J. Lough, 'The French literary underground reconsidered',
         Studies on Voltaire and the Eighteenth Century, 326 (1995). Finds
         there is not much left of the 'Grub Street' interpretation.

[117] D. Mornet, *La Pensée française au XVIIIe siècle* (1969). Contains a convenient summary of his *magnum opus* on the intellectual origins of the Revolution.
[118] D. Outram, *The Enlightenment* (1995). Excellent, lively introduction.
[119] R. Wokler, 'The Enlightenment and the French Revolutionary birth pangs of modernity', in *Sociology of the Sciences Yearbook*, vol. 20 (1996). Argues that the Revolution represented not the culmination of the Enlightenment but its end.
[120] R. Wokler, *Rousseau* (1995). The best introduction to the most important eighteenth-century political theorist, whose star is very much in the ascendant.

The New Political Culture

[121] K. M. Baker, 'Defining the public sphere in eighteenth-century France: variations on a theme by Habermas', in Craig Calhoun (ed.), *Habermas and the Public Sphere* (1992).
[122] K. M. Baker, 'Public opinion as political invention', in K. M. Baker, *Inventing the French Revolution* (1900). Sophisticated and convincing.
[123] D. Bien, 'François Furet, the Terror, and 1789', *French Historical Studies*, 16 (1990). Analyses Furet's developing interpretation of the Terror.
[124] T. E. Crow, *Painters and Public Life in Eighteenth-century Paris* (1985). Fascinating account of the formation of a 'public sphere' in the visual arts.
[125] A. Farge, *Subversive Words. Public Opinion in Eighteenth-century France* (1994). Lacks coherence but contains much interesting material.
[126] J. Habermas, *The Structural Transformation of the Public Sphere. An Inquiry into a Category of Bourgeois Society* (1989). The most important theoretical contribution; flawed by the familiar German habit of making relatively simple ideas seem enormously complex.
[127] C. Lucas (ed.), *The Political Culture of the French Revolution* (1988). Conference proceedings of variable quality, but the introduction is very useful.
[128] S. Maza, *Private Lives and Public Affairs. The Causes Célèbres of Pre-Revolutionary France* (1993). Shows that not all the literature undermining the old regime came from the gutter.
[129] B. Nathans, 'Habermas's "Public sphere" in the era of the French Revolution', *French Historical Studies*, 16, 3 (1990). Helpful exposition and critique of Habermas.
[130] M. Ozouf, 'Public opinion at the end of the old regime', *Journal of Modern History*, 60 (Supplement, September 1988), reprinted in [4].

[131]   Q. Skinner, *The Foundations of Modern Political Thought*, 2 vols (1978). A modern classic.
[132]   D. Sutherland, 'An assessment of the writings of François Furet', *French Historical Studies*, 16 (1990). A good place to start.
[133]   L. A. White, 'Culturology', *International Encyclopedia of the Social Sciences*, ed. David L. Sills, vol. III (1968). Good on anthropological definitions of culture.
[134]   R. Williams, *Culture and Society 1780–1950* (1958).

See also [7], [35], [148].

The Final Crisis

[135]   J. Égret, *The French Pre-revolution* (1977). The essential starting point for any investigation of the political crisis of the late 1780s.
[136]   S. F. Scott, *The Response of the Royal Army to the French Revolution. The Role and Development of the Line Army 1787–1793* (1978). Very important for understanding why the old regime collapsed when it did.
[137]   G. V. Taylor, 'Revolutionary and nonrevolutionary content in the *cahiers* of 1789: an interim report', *French Historical Studies*, 7 (1972). Argues persuasively that the Revolution produced the revolutionaries, not the other way around.
[138]   M. Vovelle, *The Fall of the French Monarchy 1787–1792* (1983). Intelligent but not consistently lucid defence of the Revolution as essentially bourgeois.
[139]   D. Wick, 'The court nobility and the French Revolution: the example of the Society of Thirty', *Eighteenth-Century Studies*, 13 (1980). Demonstrates the predominantly noble character of the revolutionary leadership.

The Revolution

[140]   J.-P. Bertaud, *The Army of the French Revolution: from Citizen-Soldiers to Instruments of Power* (1988). Full of interesting and surprising information.
[141]   T. C. W. Blanning, 'The French Revolution and Europe', in [9]. Places the Revolution in France in its European context.
[142]   T. C. W. Blanning, *The Origins of the French Revolutionary Wars* (1986). Examines the origins of the revolutionary wars of the 1790s, arguing that ideological differences played little part.
[143]   T. C. W. Blanning, *The French Revolutionary Wars 1787–1802* (1996). Argues that the wars and the Revolution were intertwined from the start.

[144]. H. Blömeke, *Revolutionsregierung und Volksbewegung (1793–1794). Die 'Terreur' im Departement Seine-et-Marne (Frankreich)* (1989). An excellent regional study with important general implications.

[145] A. Cobban, *Aspects of the French Revolution* (1968). Collected essays and articles; see especially (a) 'The Enlightenment and the French Revolution', (b) 'The myth of the French Revolution', (c) 'Political versus social interpretations of the French Revolution', and (d) 'The French Revolution: orthodox and unorthodox interpretations'.

[146] F. Crouzet, 'Wars, blockade and economic change in Europe 1792–1815', *Journal of Economic History*, XXIV (1964). Should be read in conjunction with [54].

[147] A. Forrest, *Society and Politics in Revolutionary Bordeaux* (1975). One of the best regional studies.

[148] F. Furet, 'Terror', in François Furet and Mona Ozouf (eds), *A Critical Dictionary of the French Revolution* (1989). Argues that the Terror was inevitable from the start.

[149] Hugh Gough, *The Newspaper Press in the French Revolution* (1988). Invaluable study of a very important dimension of revolutionary political culture.

[150] N. Hampson, *The Terror in the French Revolution* (1981). Short but penetrating pamphlet.

[151] P. Higonnet, *Class, Ideology and the Rights of Nobles during the French Revolution* (1981). Odd but stimulating.

[152] O. Hufton, 'Women in Revolution, 1789–1796', *Past and Present*, 53 (1971).

[153] O. Hufton, *Women and the limits of Citizenship in the French Revolution* (1992). Among many other things, shows how deeply involved were women in the counter-revolution.

[154] L. Hunt, *Politics, Culture and Class in the French Revolution* (1986). Not an easy read, but consistently stimulating, one of the best post-revisionist studies.

[155] L. Hunt, 'Foreword' to Mona Ozouf, *Festivals and the French Revolution* (1988). A convenient summary of a long but important book.

[156] L. Hunt (ed.), *The Invention of Pornography. Obscenity and the Origins of Modernity, 1500–1800* (1993). Hunt's own article on pornography and the French Revolution is important if overstated.

[157] P. Jones, *The Peasantry in the French Revolution* (1988). Invaluable study of a much-neglected topic.

[158] E. Kennedy, *A Cultural History of the French Revolution* (1989). Very useful.

[159] J. B. Landes, *Women and the Public Sphere in the Age of the French Revolution* (1988). Argues convincingly that women lost as a result of the Revolution.

[160]   C. Langlois and T. Tackett, 'A l'épreuve de la Révolution (1770–1830)', in F. Lebrun (ed.), *Histoire des catholiques en France du XVe siècle à nos jours* (1980). The best modern account.

[161]   G. Lewis, *The French Revolution: Rethinking the Debate* (1993). A lively critique of revisionism which asks some awkward questions.

[162]   G. Lewis, *The Second Vendée. The Continuity of Counter-revolution in the Department of the Gard 1789–1815* (1978). Fascinating account of counter-revolutionary agitation in the south-east.

[163]   M. Lyons, *France under the Directory* (1975). Organised thematically, it sheds much light on many neglected aspects of a much-neglected period.

[164]   J. McManners, *The French Revolution and the Church* (1969). Concise study of a relationship of central importance, for French readers now superseded by [160].

[165]   J. Markoff, 'Peasant grievances and peasant insurrection: France in 1789', *Journal of Modern History*, 62/3 (1990) and reprinted in [4]. Original and cogent.

[166]   M. Ozouf, 'War and terror in French revolutionary discourse (1792–1794)', *Journal of Modern History*, 56/4 (1984), reprinted in [4].

[167]   B. M. Shapiro, *Revolutionary Justice in Paris, 1789–1790* (1993). Argues that the Revolution did enjoy a liberal pluralist phase.

[168]   A. Sorel, *Europe and the French Revolution*, (1969). A true classic, first published more than a century ago, but still well worth reading especially for its emphasis on the primacy of foreign policy.

[169]   D. Woronoff, *The Thermidorian regime and the Directory 1794–1799* (1984). More chronological in organisation, it admirably complements [163].

The Aftermath

[170]   L. Bergeron, *France under Napoleon* (1981). Excellent account of the domestic side of Napoleon's empire.

[171]   M. G. Broers, *Europe under Napoleon* (1996). Excellent modern survey, containing much unusual material.

[172]   R. E. Cameron, 'Economic growth and stagnation in France 1815–1914', in B. Supple (ed.), *The Experience of Economic Growth* (1963). Examination of the problems besetting French industrialisation in the nineteenth century.

[173]   R. E. Cameron, 'A new view of European industrialisation', *Economic History Review*, 2nd series, XXXVIII (1985). Argues that the French road to industrialisation – a long slow process – was normal for Europe.

[174]   F. Crouzet, 'Les conséquences économiques de la Révolution', *Annales. Économies, Sociétés, Civilisations*, XXXIV (1962). Illustrates the detrimental consequences of the Revolution for the French economy.

[175]   G. Ellis, *The Napoleonic Empire* (1990). Concise, penetrating, comprehensive, easily the best introduction.

[176]   C. J. Esdaile, *The Wars of Napoleon* (1995). Excellent, wide-ranging account.

[177]   R. Forster, 'The French Revolution and the new elite 1800–50' in J. Pelenski (ed.), *The American and French Revolutions* (1980). Stresses the continuity of the traditional French elites.

[178]   D. R. Leet and J. A. Shaw, 'French economic stagnation 1700–1960', *Journal of Interdisciplinary History*, XCIII (1977/8). Argues that the reputation of the French economy for backwardness is undeserved.

[179]   M. Lévy-Leboyer and F. Bourguigon, *The French Economy in the Nineteenth Century* (1990).

[180]   R. Magraw, *France 1815–1914. The Bourgeois Century* (1983).

[181]   P. K. O'Brien and C. Keyder, *Economic Growth in Britain and France 1780–1914* (1978). Demonstrates, among other things, the retardative effects of the Revolution on the agrarian structure of France.

[182]   P. K. O'Brien, 'Path dependency, or why Britain became an industrialised and urbanised economy long before France', *Economic History Review*, XLIX, 2 (1996). Takes a very long view, concentrating on agriculture, geographical constraints and property rights.

[183]   P. M. Pilbeam, *The Middle Classes in Europe: France, Germany, Italy and Russia* (1990). First-rate general survey.

[184]   R. Price, *The Economic Modernisation of France* (1975). The importance of communications is the *leitmotiv* of this consistently informative and stimulating study.

[185]   R. Tombs, *France 1814–1914* (1996). A magnificent book, the best on post-revolutionary France in any language.

[186]   C. Trebilcock, *The Industrialisation of the Continental Powers 1780–1914* (1981). Excellent survey, particularly good in explaining and applying models of industrialisation.

[187]   J. Tulard, *Napoleon. The Myth of the Saviour* (1984). The best modern study; each section concludes with a helpful review of the literature and current controversies.

[188]   Eugen Weber, *Peasants into Frenchmen. The Modernisation of Rural France* (1977). A brilliant book which shows – among other things – how much of the old regime had survived into the late nineteenth century.

84

Index